I0825138

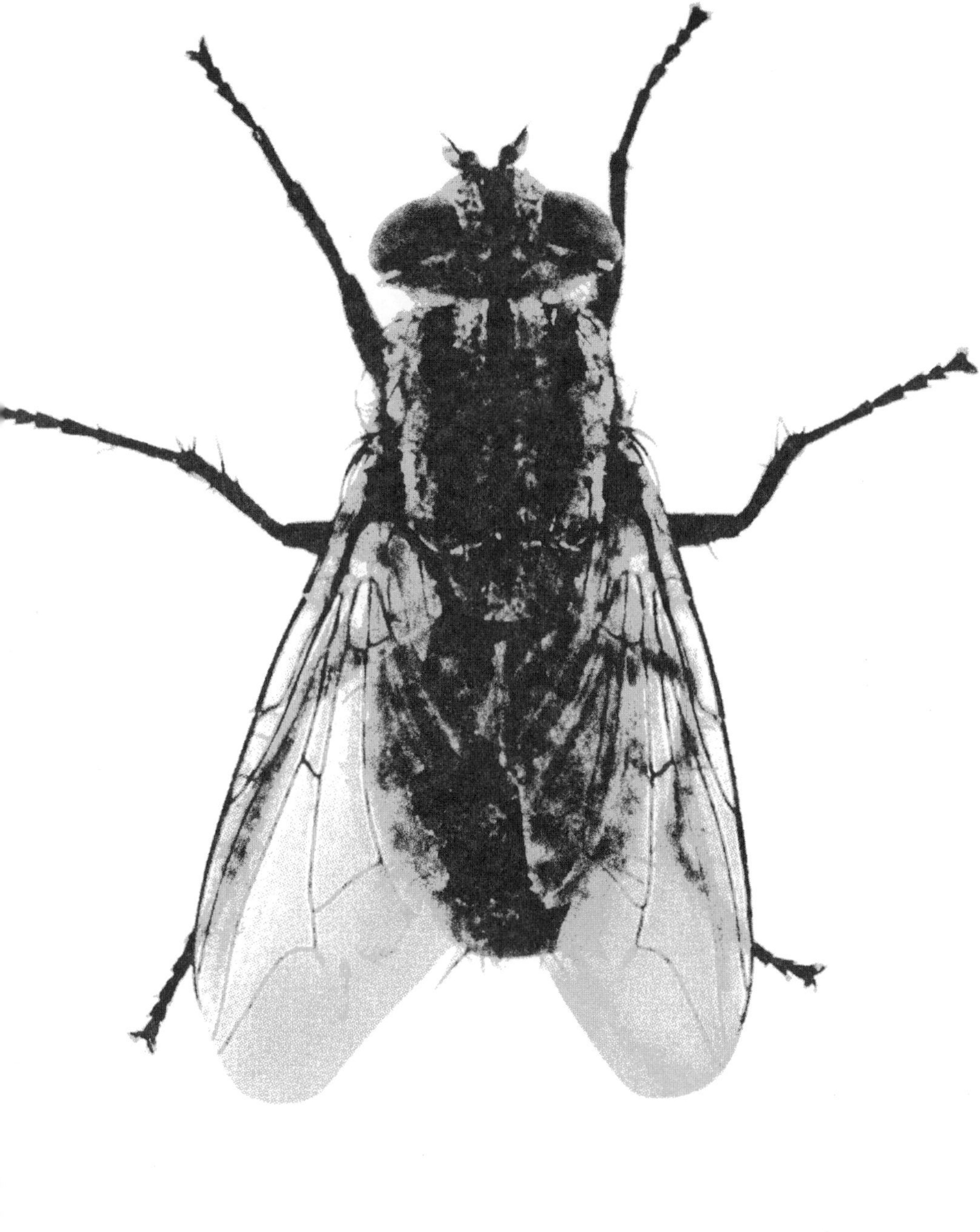

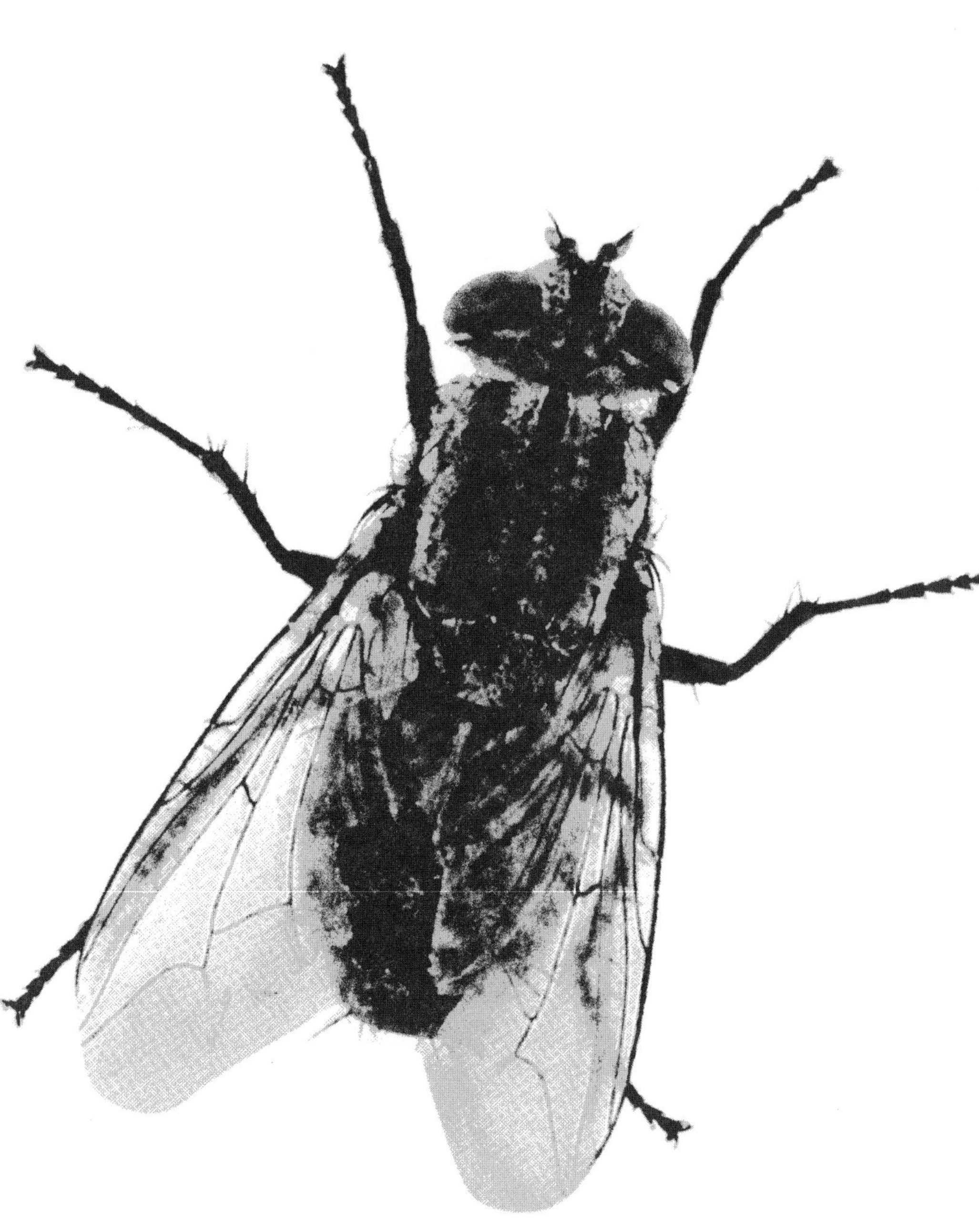

HOW TO BECOME A CHRISTIAN IN 7 DAYS*

HOW TO BECOME A CHRISTIAN IN 7 DAYS*

*May take 50 years of Sin and Serious f#ck-ups to get started

RUSSELL BRAND

TUCKER CARLSON
BOOKS

Tucker Carlson Books may be purchased in bulk at special discounts for sales promotion, corporate gifts, fund-raising, or educational purposes. Special editions can also be created to specifications. For details, contact the Special Sales Department, Skyhorse Publishing, 307 Fifth Avenue, 4th Floor, New York, NY 10016 or info@skyhorsepublishing.com.

Tucker Carlson Books is an imprint of Skyhorse Publishing, Inc.®, a Delaware corporation.

Visit our website at www.skyhorsepublishing.com.
Please follow our publisher Tony Lyons on Instagram @tonylyonsisuncertain.

10 9 8 7 6 5 4 3 2 1

Library of Congress Cataloging-in-Publication Data is available on file.

Cover design by Brian Peterson

Print ISBN: 978-1-68358-544-2
Ebook ISBN: 978-1-68358-545-9

Printed in the United States of America

I dedicate this book to Bear, my dog.
And to Jesus Christ, my God.
Both Shepherds.

“The existence of God is not subjective. He either exists or he doesn’t. It’s not a matter of opinion. You can have your own opinions. But you can’t have your own facts.”

Ricky Gervais, comedian

“For our struggle is not against flesh and blood, but against the rulers, against the authorities, against the powers of this dark world and against the spiritual forces of evil in the heavenly realms.”

Ephesians 6:12

“If God can create everything in seven days, you can create a new life with Him in seven days.”

Contents

Introduction

"I don't even understand the connection with 'died for your sins.' He died for your sin, well, how does one affect the other? 'I hit myself in the foot with a shovel for your mortgage'..."

Doug Stanhope, Comedian

When you were dead in your sins and in the uncircumcision of your flesh, God made you alive with Christ. He forgave us all our sins, having canceled the charge of our legal indebtedness, which stood against us and condemned us; he has taken it away, nailing it to the cross.

Colossians 2:13-16

"This book is for everybody" seems to me to be about the most grandiose statement any writer could make about their own work. So, we may as well start there. Not hubristically though, but from a place of brokenness and humility that I thought I'd never know.

The title of this book, *How to Become a Christian in Seven Days,* is figurative. It might take you longer, or you may already be Christian—you could, as I say, be anybody—because being Christian is not about you or even me, but about who loves us both.

I've spent, indeed it's hard not to say "wasted," my whole life trying to prize love from a loveless world on the basis of personal merits that I do not, and could not, possess.

Newly, and with a rawness that still hurts, that Love is now mine, and if one so hopeless as I can be the recipient of such Grace, then you can too.

In the Bible, the number seven means "complete" and "days" often means "distinct temporal movement"—as in Genesis's "God made the world in seven days." This cannot be intended to mean in seven twenty-four-hour periods, as of course, those periods are physically determined by the earth's rotation on its axis and the relationship between its surface and the light source around which it orbits. See, this book has already paid for itself in cosmological bullion—"Now I know what a day is!"

The book you'll ultimately have to read is the Bible; it contains the secrets of the universe and makes sense of everything, as much as things can ever really be made sense of. I mean, you could spend forever and a day quibbling about the absence of diplodocuses in Genesis or the lack of descriptions of supernovas in Leviticus, but it won't help you a jot when it comes to the more pressing problem of nagging futility at the core of your being. The Bible is the book you must read to address that, if it comes to a choice between the Bible and this humble tome, then stop reading and chuck this out of the nearest window, or into a window if you're outside. For the Bible is all about Jesus Christ, and my job is to use my experience to, *gulp,* lead you to Him. And I'll tell you now that if this doesn't make sense to you, welcome, we are in this boat, in this storm together, awaiting Him. This does not make sense in a conventional way and I am not here to demystify Christ; if anything, we must re-mystify Him.

Amidst the infinite, which is where even competing and elsewise opposed epistemologies place us, even universal laws are little more than local customs. When we say the Earth goes around the sun, which most people (but not all!) see as the basis of our galactic reality, within infinity (total unboundedness) this is about as relevant as saying, "In my house we eat Chinese food on Fridays." It may be true, but in a reality with no observable end and only a speculative beginning, it is meaningless.

"Negentropic" is the word used for the temporary and spatial "suspension" of entropy, itself the observable tendency of the molecules that make up "matter" to "move apart." This is often used to infer that we inhabit a "chaotic" reality. That there is no point to life, no point to anything. That nature contains itself and has no external inceptor, no creator. But that position requires faith too. As they say, we can't know what happened "the Tuesday before the big bang." We can't know why we live in a localized system that seems to temporarily favor order—weather and climate systems, biology, gravity, and hundreds of other necessary rules that give rise to life in opposition to, and at odds with the wider assumption of meaningless, endless expansion.

Does this make you feel that, no matter what you do or say or get or lose, human existence, life, is meaningless without God? Somehow, I've always known this and since coming to Him, since my "coming-to" period, I can handle it.

In this book, I will offer you my humble testimony—what it was like, what happened, and what it's like now. And, through my richly blessed experience in "Recovery"—the process of getting clean and sober through 12-step programs—I have attempted to address, combine, and describe a profound, involuntary, and supernatural change in my state (coming to Christ) with a reliable and repeatable technique for creating the precondition and circumstance for such a change, the 12-step system.

You see, for me it didn't take seven days or fifty years, it took an instant, an instant that He provided. He that is beyond space, time, and matter, for He created them all.

My testimony then is intercut with exercises, prayers, and questions, based on my 12-step experience—which while unique is broadly repeatable—in the hope that my conversion, which was theophanic (I just learned this word myself, don't be embarrassed, it means "God came to me") and therefore only detectable in silhouette, which by His Grace I will lapidarily (I've known this one a little longer, it means "written in stone") trace in the only form available: language. Whether written or spoken, the horror of botched translation, that only the polylinguist knows, is as nothing compared to the ascending "Bends" that clench and wring the depressurizing lobes when attempting to convert the Word of God to the language of man. So, The Word was made flesh.

My previous book, *Recovery*, contained a personal account, diagnosis, and guide to using a—forgive the word— "tool" that I can claim no credit for creating. In a way, getting off drugs is like becoming Christian. Both procedures require a type of apostasy—a rejection of one's prior faith. The faith that the best thing one can do to live in this world is to take drugs to numb, negate, and defer the weary, dreary awe of this thrilling, grilling, chilling, crushing life. The 12 steps masterly lead us out of that false belief system; this is how they sum up step 1:

> We admitted we were powerless over drugs/alcohol/whatever, and our lives had become unmanageable.

Those geniuses, of course, said "our" rather than "your" to soften the jab we feel when diagnosed so harshly as weak (powerless) and out of control (unmanageable). In *Recovery*, I abbreviated, perhaps at some cost, and no doubt with undue profanity, this elegantly composed piece of American folk prose to "Admit you're f*cked." I know, you're welcome.

It's easy to do that eventually when you're a heroin addict or a drunk. In this book, *How to Become a Christian in Seven Days*, the "tool" I am directing you to is Jesus. The apostasy I'm suggesting you undertake, having just undertaken it myself, is from the world. The world. You are not joining a religion, you are leaving one. We are not coming to faith; we are coming home.

Having cringed at my own blasphemy when attempting to interpret the 12 steps, I've shown myself a hopeless literary recidivist by committing the only heresy that could be more grievous: I'm attempting to reinterpret the Bible. All Christians do that. It's called testimony. Phew, for a minute I thought I was an out-of-control egomaniac trying to rewrite the Bible and charge you for the privilege.

When we recover from addiction, we first reject drugs and alcohol (or whatever), then, eventually the person, the "self" who is dependent upon them. The old man (or woman) must die so that we may be reborn.

Then we turn to God—as we see in the formal précis of step 2:

> We came to believe a power greater than ourselves could restore us to sanity.

I will show you how I began to see my whole reality as a type of drug and Jesus Christ as "the truth, the life and the way." We are dealing with the supernatural, which is by definition difficult to comprehend.

Someone kindly assisting me with the writing of this book suggested that my moment of epiphany, or theophany, might be compared to the moment the great chef and excellent writer Anthony Bourdain knew that he loved food. Bourdain appropriately described this sensual experience using his senses, so his enjoyment of his cherry-popping oyster becomes something like, "the lolloping, vaginal slurp and sluice of briny, unclammed and shucked oyster juice." Maybe even describing "the pinch of his new shoes" as he "neck-backed his gullet run," or "what the wallpaper was like in the restaurant." That's not literally what he wrote, that's me doing my best to write sensually, to show I can do it when it comes to mouth munchy din dins—a skill, but not the skill required here. Interfacing with the supernatural is not like a chef describing how they became a chef because eating food made them feel nice. Even though Anthony Bourdain, God rest his suicided soul, does as good a job of that as any man could. The supernatural is beyond words and beyond comprehension. Even James Joyce or Lewis Carroll in full "Jabberwocky" mode would struggle to capture the extra sensory onomatopoeia required to weave and unweave threads as fine as the shadow of smoke on a pane of light cast by a candle on a Sunday couch.

And Joyce and Carroll are alas, alack, no longer available. But we do have Saint Paul. Saint Paul says, "It may be glimpsed as if through a glass darkly." What Paul is conjuring is what one might encounter if, when looking in a mirror, one began to sense that what was looking back was breaching without piercing a barely detectable membrane, within, without, reflected, refracted, opaque and perfect—whose eyes do you suppose they are, looking back at you? Could this be Christ? We do not have an instrument to discern the flavor of this new light. The light by which all other light is seen. "Who is looking back at you from that mirror?" Saint Paul asks us. Elsewhere he is clear; indeed, it is Christ. You cannot think of yourself here. You cannot reason your way here, although Jesus is "Logos"—a supreme logical principle—the logic applied is not human, not fallen human at least. To see Him clearly we must bear His image once more. To do this, we cannot be in sin; to do this we must surrender. Then we will know "The peace which passeth all understanding," or the peace that transcends "reason."

So, by God's grace, and by the considerable work of those who have gone before, I have:

1. Put the essence of the 12 steps into a seven-day program.
2. Told my story of coming to Jesus.
3. Sorted and sourced some exercises and questions—a bit like *The Artist's Way*—which will give my testimony a structure and shape that you can follow and implement.

If you are in Christ, you already know that we seem to flicker in and out of this perfect presence; as with Paul's mirror metaphor, Christ's image is subverted by our own. If you are not in Christ, then you may begin to feel that deep down, through brokenness or unawareness, you actually worship yourself. Even if you hate yourself. We kneel at the altar of perverse self-worship and try to summon from our dead flesh something that is categorically not there.

May Christ find you.

When famous, I was an inadvertent priest and evangelist in the sick Church of our culture and its hedonistic creed. Have sex, be famous, worship yourself; what a silly boy. Maybe you are still cloistered and devoted to the culture's sick liturgy of self? You already know that it will never work, but do you know there is a way out? I am sharing it with you because that is all there is for me now. And if one as sick, wretched, and broken as I can be rescued by Him, I know you can be too.

Here is my best attempt at showing you how.

How To Become a Christian in Seven Days.

"The eye with which I see God is the same eye with which God sees me."

Meister Eckhart

And he said to me, "Son of man, eat what is before you, eat this scroll; then go speak to the people."

Ezekiel 3:1

The 12 Steps.

1. **Step 1: Honesty** – Admitting powerlessness over the addiction.
2. **Step 2: Hope** – Believing that a Power greater than ourselves can restore us.
3. **Step 3: Faith** – Deciding to turn our will and lives over to the care of God (as understood by the individual).
4. **Step 4: Courage** – Making a searching and fearless moral inventory of ourselves.
5. **Step 5: Integrity** – Admitting to God, ourselves, and another human being the exact nature of our wrongs.
6. **Step 6: Willingness** – Becoming entirely ready to have God remove all these defects of character.
7. **Step 7: Humility** – Humbly asking Him to remove our shortcomings.
8. **Step 8: Love (or Brotherly Love)** – Making a list of all persons we had harmed and becoming willing to make amends.
9. **Step 9: Discipline (or Justice)** – Making direct amends to such people wherever possible.

10. **Step 10: Perseverance** – Continuing to take personal inventory and promptly admitting when we are wrong.
11. **Step 11: Spirituality** – Seeking through prayer and meditation to improve our conscious contact with God.
12. **Step 12: Service** – Having had a spiritual awakening, carrying this message to others and practicing these principles in all our affairs.

The First Day: Honesty

In the beginning:

"The Christian ideal has not been tried and found wanting. It has been found difficult; and left untried."

G.K. Chesterton

Do you not know that your bodies are temples of the Holy Spirit, who is in you, whom you have received from God? You are not your own.

1 Corinthians 6:19

You feel it, too. The world is changing fast, too fast, and people are waking up with a start. Was it the pandemic? Partly. The death of Charlie Kirk? Somewhat. Renewed hostility in the Middle East? Is it technology? Minneapolis? The dreadful and bilious sense that every single bloody event causes conflict and conflagration? Even Bad Bunny dancing in a hedge at the Super Bowl brings the whole hollow culture to the brink. As Andrew Lawrence says, "The reason there is no harmony is because there is no melody." Whether you are an atheist, a Muslim, or a Jew, you know that we are on the edge of a Great Revival, and you likely know there isn't much time. This is the quickening, the reckoning. The awakening. Maybe even "the Second Coming is at hand" and the reason you're reading this book is because you know we need to be Reborn.

Your life is broken, and you are broken.

Now, the last thing I wanted to be is a Christian. I've met Christians and I've seen them on the television. To me it seems that they're either inept, sexless, and drab or so far the other way—intense, swivel-eyed, and that even if they don't have halitosis, it sort of seems like they must. I can smell it through the screen.

The American ones spend too much time on their hair and the English ones not enough.

They all seem like they're trying to tell you or sell you something.

The American ones keep getting caught with their pants down and the English ones seem like they've nothing going on in their pants.

The American ones seem like they're using the Bible as a weapon, a leather-bound baton of bigotry, and the English ones are so weak-tea-gray-probably-gay-bad-teeth-tedious that, well, hell don't seem so bad.

I mean do you remember (f*ckin') *Songs of Praise*? If you're American, please allow me to describe this televisual anti-propaganda, and tell you plain that if you were like people across Iraq right now, mysteriously encountering Christ in dreams, because the culture there tries to hide him, *Songs of Praise* would spin you one hundred and eighty degrees in the opposite direction. They made the Son of God as appealing as a cat-tongue enema. Let me unpack it: Every Sunday evening, as dreadful and inevitable as the tap of a ghoulish stepdad upon your bedroom door, this Mardi Gras of grayness would unfurl. "This week we're in Rochester, Kent at St. Michael's Cathedral and by the end of this half hour, we aim to convince you that the Creator of the universe coming to earth as a baby and being nailed to a cross to absolve your personal shame is as interesting as filling in a spreadsheet of household expenses for a neighbor you dislike."

I also heard all about Jesus at school, how kind He was, and loving, and that He was the son of God and the reason we have Easter, Christmas and, come to that, secular humanitarianism. And I must say, I was unable separate the Holy Water from the bath water. So, I quickly learned not to trust anyone, or anything, based on reliable evidence and experience. You can't trust school. You can't trust TV. You can't really even trust family. In fact, the first part of being Christian came to me for free: Reject the world.

Reject its systems, reject its ways, its patterns. I was shown that the world, its culture, and all its systems are bullsh*t. A trick, a distraction, a scam. It is the counterfeit world of the evil one, though I wouldn't have framed it that way then. That took time. I dedicated myself to getting a better deck chair on the Titanic, instead of what I should've done—investigate who funded the Titanic and whether they actually ever intended for it to reach New York. Certainly, some very powerful interests benefitted from its "unsinkable" sinking. That happens a lot with crises, I've noticed. What's a crisis for us is a boon time for the world's most powerful elites.

I wonder what patterns that dichotomy might generate!? "They"* (we'll get into "they" later) primarily want to dim, diminish, vanquish, or at least redirect your spirit, your personal power. Consider that within you (did you know?) there is a portion of the divine, shooting, roaming, spreading, and searching, and the function of the world is to entice, enchant, wrap, and shellac it, a new and choking womb. Enclosed in self. Trapped on an inward ricochet of solipsistic inner circuitry, caroming endlessly in here with constant wants and fears. The famed and ubiquitous "inner voice" (Who is this inner tormentor?), the relentless monologue of intermittent loathing and megalomania: "I'm fantastic." "I'm awful." "I'm the piece of shit around which the world revolves." How did it get in there? Is it even possible to live another way?

I am broken. Are you broken? You're not too clever, messed up or addicted, New Age or atheistic to turn "your life" over to Jesus. I want you to see why we need a spiritual experience. Why the world has prevented us from having one, and why Jesus is the only answer. If you're already Christian, you may marvel at how slow I've been to get to the party but at least I'm here now and I've brought a bottle. If you're one of the many people who frequently tell me that they've been praying for me, thank you and God bless you. It worked.

Now that I am a Christian (still shocks me) I know that I am no better than you in the eyes of the One who matters, and I am no worse than you. He has no favorites and He would have come to Earth and died on the cross just as easily and readily if you (or I, makes no difference to Him) had been the only person in the world.

"The creator of the simulation came and entered the simulation to show us how to survive, how to actually 'be' in the simulation."

The definitive Christian idea is that God came to Earth and lived a human life, Jesus of Nazareth. He "went around doing good," then, and this is an understatement, necessarily died on the cross to reconcile man to God. We can imagine this, thanks to accelerating technology as a "simulation," a reality that has been constructed, or caused by a creator, who created us, only to enjoy and love us, that we might love Him. In the Bible we see how our necessary "free will" (for without it, what would be the point in creation?) led to sin. We, in the story of Adam and Eve, chose to be disobedient. We used our free will to activate self-will. Sin is not the act, it is the spiritual state that precedes the act. That is why Christ says, "If you look lustfully upon a woman you have committed adultery." The supreme level of reality is not, as we assume, the material, the plane of action, but the "spiritual" plane of the ineffable (to us) spirit. Throughout the Old Testament, God's chosen people are disobedient. They ignore, denigrate, and annoy God's prophets and leaders until he has to reset reality himself, not with a punitive flood, but through redeeming blood. He himself must through His son achieve reconciliation with us, His supreme creation. To stop humans saying, "We can't do this, it's too hard." He incarnated, brought into matter and flesh the Holy frequency that meant that less brokerage, more direct access than ever was viable. Through His atoning sacrifice on the cross. Now we live in a superstate of potentiality where we can either join Him, by collapsing our self-will, as Christ did—and as Mary, to a lesser degree, did—or we can, like Eve and Adam, reactivate our particular self-will. We still have a choice but it's easier than it used to be and it's open to all of us. When you read the Bible you will see that this applies to you. That the Bible is the voice of God and has infinite application. You will see music, geometry, and math threaded throughout the Word; indeed, the very existence of music, geometry, and math tells us that there is absolute meaning beyond subjectivity. These are the visible products of the embedded code. A code that we are not equipped to fully know because we are not God but we can be co-heirs with His Son. Our hardware is limited; His software is not.

When you only know your own pain and pleasure, in the end you feel like this:

The edges are closing in, you can feel it everywhere. Now I am a little bit dumb; I'm a fast thinker but a slow learner. I need big, clear, vivid lessons to absorb even the most basic facts. But like you, I was made for worship, and I never had a problem with that. Sometimes the love courses through me so quickly and so thickly that I feel like I could die. Man, I loved women. Man, I loved drugs. Man, I thought I knew a whole lot about everything; I thought I knew what was in the Bible based on a few trips to drab churches and a "one eye open" squint at daytime Charlton Heston movies. I did not consider Christianity to be a place where I might encounter the mystery—the mystery of my emptiness, the mystery of my loss, the mystery of precipitous awe, the gurgling and visceral need in me for comfort and love. No, not till sixteen and LSD and UFOs and Alex Jones did those queer inklings find a fuzzy and impermanent home. Not till Jung's *Red Book* and *Siddhartha* or *Autobiography of a Yogi* did I begin to see that yes indeed there is more to this than me and what I want and don't want. Not till I was cracked and smacked then uncracked and unsmacked and therapized and had been through Sartre and sutras and Nietzsche and sex creatures, until I'd turned my childhood shame into adult fame, only for that fame to metastasize once more into shame, only when I saw the false idols of sex and fame like two serpents, like two coiled helices turn with Murdoch's venom, in foul and Faustian disgrace; *"Oh, so you want to be famous do you? And have lots of sex? How about being portrayed as THE MOST FAMOUS RAPIST IN THE WORLD? Ah Ha ha ha ha HA ha..."*

And as the idol cracked open, as the serpent burst forth, as my son's chest was carved open, as my wife's breast milk bloomed, as we left the anesthesiologist's room, as the dog leash loomed, a casual and accessible noose flung across the beam in the garage, as the paparazzi gathered like locusts at the end of the lane, amidst the offers of late-term abortion and fake accusation and the faces of longtime friends melted into blank and empty stares, as the snares snapped shut, in the twisting of the gut, the portcullis fell and the long awaited dread arrived, as the final hope that this world could ever deliver died, there He was.

At first, not even our Lord. At first it was His cross.

While walking the dog. My German Shepard, Bear.

On flat flood plains he makes me lie down in green pastures, by the Thames he leads me beside quiet waters. He refreshes my soul. He guides me along the right paths,

Even though I walk through a dark valley, carved by time, by glacial time, like the scourges on His back, like the flies on His back, like iron filings pulled by a magnet across time, in the silent constant fog of my suicidal mind, in the shadow of death, in the grey, in the trudge of the tedious day, my mate Ralph (Ralph from NA?!) sent a clip of Rick Warren on some televangical smiling show with blonded host, husband and wife all teeth and tax breaks and Rick Warren unremarkable and rounded, bearded, and never-seen-by-me-before plainly explains his son's suicide without self-pity or false pride and my "oh so agile" mind is met at last by You, Lord, my Christ, my glorious Christ.

And I sit now by the top field where Bear had gored sheep the winter before. Blood on snow. And in the valley, Lord, in the shadow of death, Yours, Lord, not mine, I saw Your cross as you took my hand, my gracious King, and you have held it since. I don't know if I cried then, but I weep now, God, to feel once more how lonely and how broken I was by febrile and foolish worship, and how hard I had clung to the graven images of my precious culture and my precious place in it: famous.

Day One: Honesty

> *In the beginning God created the heavens and the earth. Now the earth was formless and empty, darkness was over the surface of the deep, and the Spirit of God was hovering over the waters.*
>
> *And God said, "Let there be light," and there was light. God saw that the light was good, and he separated the light from the darkness. God called the light "day," and the darkness he called "night." And there was evening, and there was morning—the first day.*
>
> Genesis 1:1 NIV

When all reality was created you were created too. There was an ultimate reality (heaven) and an expressed reality (earth). Light came after vibration, God in wave form created the particular by speaking light into being. Through light we can see, whether we envisage that as photons or awareness. You must know the truth of your condition. In sin, we are 'dead men walking.' Can you awaken to the need for Christ in your life? Do you feel formless, empty and dark? God is hovering just above you.

Here are some questions to consider:

Do you admit that your life is not working?

That we must admit we are in crisis?

That we are not drowning, we are dead in the water?

You've read the first part of my testimony. And, this is no small thing, *you've lived your whole life up until this point.* Let's level with each other; *it's not working is it?*

The good things and the bad things, the whole thing. Being you and being me is not enough and it will never be enough.

It was never supposed to be. You trying to get happiness out of yourself in this world is like trying to get "blood out of a stone" or a self-effacing remark out of Trump. Or, just to show that this is way beyond politics, a cogent answer out of Biden—or, if the news is to be believed (and it isn't), a signature.

Please honestly admit to yourself at least three things that are causing you pain and suffering in the space below.

(I'm an old hand at this. I could do this with Joe Biden's autopen, and I've not even thought about these examples):

- My children will die.
- I am getting old.
- No matter what happens in court, such as acquittal, or the evident presence of malign power, some people will always think I'm a rapist.
- I can never take drugs again.
- What if my wife leaves me?

It came so easily, I literally had to stop myself typing.

Now you. Take a breath, pray:

> *"Lord, if you're Real, help me to put aside all of my preconceptions about You and myself and write down what bothers me."*

Now that you have done this, if you can stand to, look into a mirror and pause, breathe a while, at least two minutes, and admit: "I cannot do this alone anymore."

When you have done this, please spend a few minutes in the company of someone who loves you. If there is no one, then please know that I love you, and more importantly, He does and He is here now.

Here we conclude The First Day.

The Second Day: Hope

Separate water from water

"The first gulp from the glass of natural sciences will turn you into an atheist, but at the bottom of the glass God is waiting for you."

Werner Heisenberg, Quantum Physicist

That day when evening came, he said to his disciples, "Let us go over to the other side."

Mark 4:35

I invite you to consider our quandary the way an alcoholic or addict must learn to view their addiction. We are locked into a pattern that we cannot break. A behavior that plainly has a neurological correlative. Now I'm not an expert in much, but I am an expert in addiction. This is what I know: The addict is attempting to synthesize a divine experience, trying to defibrillate dead matter through chemical infusion. Like the episode of *The Simpsons* in which Homer is mistaken for a maker of contemporary sculpture ("but, then again, no") by a passing art critic (it's a cartoon!) and then must repeat the trick. Homer batters a piece of steel with a hammer yelling, "Why won't you be art?!" at the recalcitrant piece. All my life I've been trying to make matter divine, to make it luminous with the numinous, but matter ain't like that; it's moving apart across time and unless a new yuga redolent with Holy and incandescent glow commences, that ain't gonna change.

Here is how the problem of addiction is described in a rich and vital correspondence between Alcoholics Anonymous founder Bill W and father of psychology and modern mystic Carl Jung. In this exchange, famous amongst 12-step nerds, Bill W credits Jung with spontaneously concocting the "molecular formulation" of AA. When Jung hit Roland Hazard, an alcoholic under his care, who had been most recalcitrant and unresponsive to treatment, with a harsh prognosis: "You are doomed. You're hopeless and you're going to die from your alcoholism." Almost as a *Columbo*-style afterthought, Jung, who if nothing else trusted his intuition, said there may be a slim hope if his patient

1. Had a profound spiritual experience, which we might call an "awakening" or even an "epiphany."
2. Continued to receive the ongoing support of a like-minded and invested community.

These two components, by the reckoning of AA founder Bill W, are the foundational principles of AA and therefore all 12 step–oriented recovery programs. It is also notable that Bill W considered Jung's personal declaration that he could be of no further assistance to his former patient as of considerable value, too; insomuch as it represented a threshold that remains significant within AA: "That no human power could relieve us of our dilemma," with Jung in this instance providing a plausible apex for human power, particularly in the field of psychoanalysis, that to this day remains to some a viable alternative to religious faith.

In Carl Jung's response to Wilson's admiring letter, he wrote: "His craving for alcohol was the equivalent, on a low level, of the spiritual thirst of our being for wholeness, expressed in medieval language: the union with God."

"As the deer panteth after the water brooks, so panteth my soul after thee, O God." Psalms 42:1

It excites me as an alcoholic and drug addict that Jung so readily equated chemical dependency and misuse with a "spiritual thirst" and as a Christian that he reached for Psalm 42 as the scriptural compound that demonstrated his point.

Jung continues: "How could one formulate such an insight in a language that is not misunderstood in our days?"

I am intrigued that Jung so quickly observed that the culture of the twentieth century was already skeptical when discussing "spiritual experiences." Until literally eighteen months ago, when there seemed to me to be an inexplicable lurch towards religion—indeed, I consider my own conversion to be part of a global revival that I alluded to at the start of this book—the trend towards rationalism, materialism, and even atheism was continuing, apace. To note that the near advent of psychotherapy, and towards the end of his life, one of its founders acknowledged the necessity for Faith. In this context, for the treatment of serious addiction, but as we will explore, the diagnostics, language, and solution outlined here may help us understand the failure of secularism and to facilitate the return to Christ that is a personal and cosmic solution.

But it is what Jung says next that I would like to leverage in persuading you to spark, light, or reignite your own relationship with Jesus. Jung appears to conclude that a supernatural evil entity, an organized, demonic intelligence is in control of the world, an idea with which any well-versed Christian or even a semi-committed conspiracy theorist will be most familiar, when he says: "I am strongly convinced that the evil principle prevailing in this world leads the unrecognized spiritual need into perdition, if it is not counteracted either by real religious insight or by the protective wall of human community. An ordinary man, not protected by an action from above and isolated in society, cannot resist the power of evil, which is called very aptly the Devil."

Now, I must cop to my nerdiness here; for me, correspondence between Bill W and Carl Jung is like eavesdropping on the meeting between Elvis and The Beatles. Or Biggie and Tupac, or Watson and Crick, or Noam Chomsky and Stephen Hawkings at Cabana Bar on Epstein Island —if they could even talk with their mouths full. Here we have the "patient zero" of alcoholism, the great Bill W, a man with an ego the size of a continent who by faith and guidance was able to found an anonymous organization and keep money and credit out of it, intimately communing with the man that kept the mystery of human consciousness and spirit alive in psychoanalysis, when his collaborator Sigmund Freud would've reduced our numinous yet knowable souls into naught but hopeless hankerings after incest and cocaine. Freud's psychoanalysis in the end is reducible to fretful perversions and repressed fantasy, reifying the sexual instinct as both the highest human experience and the source of all malady. Believe me—I bought a ticket to that donkey derby and it doesn't end well. Both Wilson and Jung discovered and explained that beyond the explicable catastrophes that may afflict a man, whether from extreme mental illness or extreme substance misuse, is the unmet need for God. A moral God, a real God within to comfort and a God without to establish immutable moral standards—and this at a time where an apparent global plan to demolish God and replace Him with state authority was reaching near invincibility.

Jung says that "An evil principle is prevailing in this world . . ." and goes on to say that "The power of evil" may as well be called "the devil."

Once, as I was departing one of those self-help meetings that you get these days, where the principles of the twelve steps fuse with the principles of the Church—one example being "Celebrate Recovery"—I sidled up to a fella to whom I had inclined, as I often do within these rooms, on hearing people, eyes middle-distance fixed, dreamily declare their fascinating, idiosyncratic but recognizable wrongs, the heartbreak and hopelessness, the messy marriages and soiled trousers, the broken childhoods and warped thinking, and asked him, "As an addict and a Christian, which metaphor do you consider to be more apt when describing your condition: the preferred 12-step moniker 'disease,' or the Christian personification of evil, 'the devil?' After but a moment of reflection, this lay practitioner of heathen metaphysics responded, "The devil," with eerie certainty. He continued. "Because it's a planned, organized, evil intelligence." I liked the verdict and the phrase so much that I've just plagiarized it in this book. It resonated with me in the same way Jung's earlier words do—"Evil principle prevailing in this world . . ." Haven't you always known that evil was real? Haven't you stopped short, perhaps through fear of being judged, from screaming outright, "The devil is alive and well and living in D.C. (or Westminster or Davos or Jerusalem)?" Isn't it obvious now why human excellence is everywhere repressed and human beauty denigrated? Why our food is poisoned at the point of manufacture? Why companies charged with medical responsibility actually do harm? Why the institutions that are meant to convey truth deceive and lie? Why the function of government has become to control rather than to serve? Why commerce has become maximally exploitative? Why children are being sexualized?

It is because the devil is in charge of this world.

This is not just my intuition and personal observation. Consider this, from the gospel of Luke, where at the commencement of His ministry our Lord is tempted by Satan, to ensure he's up to the job.

> "The devil led him up to a high place and showed him in an instant all the kingdoms of the world. And he said to him, 'I will give you all their authority and splendor; it has been given to me, and I can give it to anyone I want to. If you worship me, it will all be yours.'" Luke 4:5-7 NIV

The devil led him to a "high place." I consider this to be a kind of transcendent, psychedelic superstate, rather than a hill, mountain or topographical high. I believe that the reason that it is "In an instant" is because a dialogue between "God as man" and, to use Jung's phrase, "The evil principle prevailing in this world" is an exchange outside of and beyond time. Here too is the scriptural statement, one of many, that from a Biblical position, worldly power belongs to the devil;

> "I will give you the authority, it has been given to me, and I can give it to anyone I want to."

Perhaps you think that using the Bible to prove the existence of the devil or God is like using DC Comics to prove the existence of Batman and the Penguin. But do you feel the chill that claims me? The inward affirmation on reading this? The ancient explanation of worldly evil, in your life and at large? The haunting sense that world has become so wretched might be because the devil is eternally making this offer and Christ repudiates eternally. Not so with fallen humans like you and I though. When the devil makes the offer that he made to Christ to mortals, we do not cite scripture and ascend towards the Father, no. Most accept the dreadful pact. We have been trained for our whole lives to believe that when the offer of worldly power comes it is the highest bid that we will receive. We have been blinded and don't even see the offer as external "temptation" but as a natural, inner fulfilment of necessary, rational goals. It's what we are supposed to do. Be yourself. Just do it. You're worth it. Become who you are, according to the mad metrics of this broken, fallen world. Accept the devil's offer and worship the dumb idols of money and fame and sex, pursue it, actively or vicariously. Many of our most adored heroes have at some point made this pact. Only Christ has perfectly refuted it. Likely you, like me, have made your own version of this diabolical contract without even noticing it. The most malign and effective power doesn't even appear to be power at all, just a chance to conform to the pattens of this world.

Here is a surprising scriptural rendering of this subtle form of false idolatry. It's one of the first verses that really grabbed me, not because someone had pointed it out or explained it, although I of course have plenty of those to refer to. This is one of the first examples of the Word speaking to me. Again, it is from the Gospel of Luke. Here the seventy-two disciples have returned from an early mission, casting out demons, and healing and such. When they gleefully, if a little hubristically, inform our Lord Jesus of their adventures and triumphs, he says, "I saw Satan fall like lightning from heaven. I have given you authority to trample on snakes and scorpions and to overcome all the power of the enemy; nothing will harm you. However, do not rejoice that the spirits submit to you, but rejoice that your names are written in heaven." Luke 10;18.NIV

Why does His admonishment begin with this extraordinary claim of witness to the fall of Lucifer? Who would make such a thing up? Why does this "man" Jesus make reference to seeing this weird, eerie, mythic, historic, mystical and trippy moment when Satan fell from Heaven? It is because these effective, yet inflated missionaries have committed the very sin that Satan did, the sin which caused Satan to fall from Heaven, from grace, from the absolute, to separate, before there was an Adam and Eve, or even an Eden, this Satan had fallen. Why? What did he do and why does Christ mention it now? Christ teaches in time, through time, and here uses the opportunity of inadvertent but definite hubris to illustrate to His followers that Satan, and sin itself, is defined by the tendency to claim authority and power over your own life and actions apart from God. The false belief that you created yourself and that you belong to yourself and that you can do what you want with your life. All sin begins in self, not with transgression of action but with transgression of perspective, with the breach beyond the Holy Flow of His Eternal Grace, His absolute presence and "non separateness" from you. Satan fell from grace and from heaven because he believed, like I do sometimes, like you may, when infected by his essential contagion that we are sovereign. And as every TV commercial instructs, and as the enlightenment posits, and as Instagram unthinkingly demands; I am the apex, the zenith of all creation, that I am as a god, that I can do what I want. That "Do what thou wilt is the whole of the law." Now to be fair to Aleister Crowley (the filthy satanist who coined that crazy satanic mantra), his philosophy of "Thelema" did include the idea that "Will," when perfectly practiced under the law of love, would tend towards a kind of cosmic harmony. And, to be fair to "The Enlightenment," many of the key ideas like primacy of reason, natural rights, and the social contract, had benefits. Notably, and this is no small achievement—WESTERN CIVILIZATION—but, and it's a big, significant but (one less 't' but a lot more clout than even, I dunno, Megan Thee Stallion's butt), all the best aspects of Enlightenment Philosophy are already in Christianity and the biggest failings are a result of deviation from it. Although I will concede that God didn't directly give us telescopes or microscopes, just the minds to conceive of them and the eyes to use them.

Here's how ChatGPT, that plaything of Beelzebub, surmises these key Enlightenment tenets:

> "Enlightenment thinkers believed that human reasoning and empirical evidence, rather than religious dogma or superstition, were the primary sources of knowledge and truth. This

confidence in reason led to the development of the scientific method and a surge of scientific inquiry."

The scientific method and scientific inquiry are pretty fantastic things, but anyone who's lived through a pandemic, will surely recognize it's fallibility and its limits—and that's all of us, except for those who died in it, or erm, after it due to, erm, the MRNA "Vaccines"that were so effective that:

- We had by means of propaganda, threats, and out-and-out lies, to be compelled to take them.
- They had to rewrite the dictionary so the word vaccine meant what they now needed it to mean.
- They secured legal indemnity prior to using their experimental and in some cases lethal product.

Any of you detecting the potential presence of "planned evil intelligence" in the itinerary above should at once check yourself into the David Icke Sanitarium for The Conspiratorially Insane. And please don't read any of the Epstein file correspondence between the eponymous Jeffrey and Bill Gates because it looks like they were discussing and even planning a global pandemic, lockdown, and vaccine roll-out before any of us knew where Wuhan was or what Spike Protein meant.

I never took them myself, as a natural rebel when it comes to human authority, especially the government and the media, due to, well, being alive for a while. I'm aware of the irony that when addicted to heroin I was quite willing to take Gritty's (my crack and heroin dealer) dubious merchandise without FDA approval or due sanitation but those were different times, and anyway, I'd still trust Gritty over Pfizer. Frankly, my disobedience saved me when it came to Covid vaccines and their interminable "boosters" (boosters? What were they boosting other than Moderna profits and male infertility? Them boosters kept coming, and when you thought they were expired, here comes another one, like Kardashians).

If the government had really wanted me to take those shots all they had to do was hide one somewhere in my house and tell me under no circumstances was I to touch it. I'd have had it injected into my optic nerve within an hour.

Before we conclude Jung's eerie foretelling of this extraordinary revival that you and I are now a part of, here are a few more scriptural allusions to and descriptions of Satan's dominion over the Earth. For material evidence of the Evil One's control over culture please, download X, scroll down for fifteen seconds—that should give you all the proof you need.

After His betrayal by Judas (whatever happened to that guy?), Jesus prepared to hand himself over to human authority, both the Pharisee priest class that effectively governed the first-century Jews culturally and the Romans that governed them militarily, He said:

> "I will not say much more to you, for the prince of this world is coming. He has no hold over me." John 14:30

I was surprised to see that throughout the New Testament he paradigm we are invited to use when understanding the nature of this world is one of conflict and tension between good and evil in which we are active participants. The current culture war provides a futile approximation of the real spiritual warfare in which we are all participants.

If you followed my career when I was working in contemporary Babylon's soft propaganda wing, a.k.a. Hollywood, you may be aware that I was a stand-up comedian, you may even know that I made a blasphemous show called: *Messiah Complex*, in which I compared myself to Jesus Christ as well as Malcolm X, Che Guevara, and Gandhi. It was actually pretty funny, aside from the heresy.

A huge part of my reluctance to follow Jesus was that I wanted to be Jesus. This is not as ridiculous as it sounds nor as uncommon as it ought be. Look again at Luke 10:18: Isn't Satan's defining and essential sin that he wants to be God? I wanted to be the epicenter of my own life, master of my domain. As much as I resisted the divine aspect of Christ, it was my resistance to the "fully man" aspect of our Lord that is perhaps most telling. I don't want to bow down in front of a man (steady), I don't want to take the knee and pledge obedience before a man. I don't trust men. Men have hurt me badly. Most of the times I've been beaten up or degraded it's been at the hands of men. Indeed, and I mean this with all due respect to my own dad, the idea of an ever-present Father who loves me more than I can comprehend or requite is enough to choke me. I've been conditioned to withhold my trust from men and to regard fathers with deep suspicion. And I grew up in the eighties and nineties, before men were subject to vindictive and ubiquitous condemnation. Almost everywhere you look in our culture, men are portrayed badly. They're corrupt patriarchs, they're sexual predators, they're pedophiles, they're hypocrites and racists, they're absent and abusive fathers, they're manspreading, mansplaining, woman-hating monsters.

Lord help the recipients of that cultural message, regardless of their sex. That's two aspects of the Trinity that I'm not gonna go anywhere near in a hurry—the Son and the Father—and the third, the Holy Ghost, is by His nature, somewhat ineffable. Why not then yield to the inarguable creed of our culture and worship yourself? Worship fame and money and sex and pleasure? Why not create mystical and altered states through chemicals and sex? Why not glorify the self, be ambitious for the self? It seems so plausible when you're in it, too. All the attention and approval, the laughs, the orgasms, the billboards with your face on them, the headlines with your name in them, the perfect salve to a deep and permanent sense of loss and separation, of hopeless exile.

When you are a cherished artifact of the culture it seems somehow warranted: "No wonder I'm having all this sex and making all this money and having people stare agog at my spontaneous opining—I am, after all The Most Important Thing in the World." Of course, I didn't recognize that my credit from the culture was an almost inadvertent consequence of the role that I'd been unwittingly cast to play in it; bad-boy hedonist, cheeky Brit, sex-mad bohemian, living endorsement of promiscuity and aspartame narcissism. Again, I thought, "The Most Important Thing in the World." And, "I deserve this after everything I've been through" (tough childhood, addiction etc.).

I first noticed that the value of a public figure is assigned on the basis of their utility in the new firmament when reading Yuval Noah Harari's admittedly excellent book *Sapiens*. Which, if you've been living under a rock, or more likely, staring at a screen, is an articulate appraisal of our species' condition as creatures who literally (for what reason not even Harari can tell you) make up meaning. Therefore, our shared destiny lies, he says, in the hands of those most currently adept at imposing centralized control. He foresees and recommends a future in which an infinitely empowered and centralized state exerts, through technology, total bio-control.

Sapiens is an anthropological history that, through its conclusion that there is no God, ultimately advocates for "a New World Order." It is Barack Obama's favorite book. Project 2030: "You will own nothing and you will be happy;" "Eat the bugs;" "Wear the mask;" "Take the vax;" "support the war;" "Pay the tax;" "Digital ID;" "Free speech is not hate-speech;" "Misinformation;" "Disinformation;" "Malinformation;" "Our information" Globalist imperial order, all these happy globalist creeds hang upon the ideas that Harari explains so well in his, again, well-written, Obama-adored manifesto.

The first part of *Sapiens* is great. Harari explores and explains how we can create flags, logos, icons, and meaning to generate cohesive stories that enable us to profit as groups or tribes of increasing size.

Whether it's a car company, like Peugeot, or a Neolithic plan to catch a mammoth, a nation's flag or, you guessed it, a religion, according to Harari (and, coincidentally, anyone who's seriously interested in impermeable power) what distinguishes homo sapiens from rats or pigs or the many obsolete humanoids that he's certain we bludgeoned to death (based on faith) is our ability to just "make stuff up" and pretend it's true. Now, even if that idea appeals to you, and it's a key facet of atheism of course, just for a moment consider Lucius Cassius Longinus Ravilla's timeless inquiry "*Cui bono*?" or in English, "Who benefits?" The answer is: Any institute or system determined to ensure its own total power by denying the existence of any other source of authority.

"If men don't believe in God, it doesn't mean they'll believe in nothing but that they'll believe in anything," is how Catholic writer G. K. Chesterton is said to have termed the precondition for the modern paganism for which Harari evangelizes.

I interviewed Harari several times before my own exile from Babylon and he was actually very nice, and it was many years later that it was explained that Harari is the World Economic Forum founder (and "slobbering Santa Claus of the New Order") Klaus Schwaab's "Go to" intellectual. What can we infer from that? It was a professional in-person encounter with Harari that helped me to understand the potentially deadly intent of the sterile and "friendly seeming" globalist system that, in one way or another, deploys all public figures to amplify various aspects of its ideology. Harari invites you to submit to the inevitability of a centralized and sanitized New World Order, to comfortably depend on it. It's going to happen, it's inert and in motion, so just let it consume you like invading olfactory water as you snugly concede to drowning.

This kindly, friendly, inevitable Kafkaesque globalist system wants total control, which is not possible if you have a significant number of people who know that the highest possible authority is God and that we, all of us, are His. They must deny the existence of God and normalize individual authority. This can be brilliantly masked as individual human rights but becomes in practice ubiquitous self-centeredness, everyone independently worshipping themselves, maybe via their maleness or femaleness or blackness or whiteness; the system doesn't care as long as your god and your self are one. When I understood that this is also what Satan wants, I saw that the Christian perspective is a bulwark and shield against evil, and that is why it is denigrated and denied. The globalist system is satanic. Satan deals in counterfeits. Observe how the globalist state's intention is to achieve omniscience through surveillance. Hmmmm. And omnipresence through online technology. Hmmmm. And omnipotence through digital ID and the control of finance, movement and information that yields. Hmmmmm. Now, as they say, all these systems are being put in place for your convenience or safety, your comfort or your protection.

Witness beneath the sanitary Huxleyian, Steve Jobs-slick-gleam the hideous archetype of the devouring mother, or of Saturn devouring his children, or the whore of Babylon who offers endless comfort and pleasure. In the previous century, the demonic movements that wanted total control were at least obvious about it: big shiny boots, red and black flags, eye-catching mustaches. These days, the fascists and the tyrants are trying to bore us into submission in a lukewarm bath of totalitarianism. I never thought I'd say this but Hitler is quaint by comparison. Shouting, spitting, doing amphetamine and annexing at will. You knew where you stood with that guy. Probably not too close to him. Or the Eastern Front. And best to keep the conversation to dogs and make sure to have some meth on you in case he went on a downward swing.

Dictators these days come with a smile, an offer to protect you, and a 90 percent safe and effective vaccine. And all you have to do is whatever they tell you, forever.

Even in its beta phase this omniscient, omnipresent, omnipotent, centrally orchestrated technocratic dystopia is obviously a counterfeit of God's Power. Secularism effectively denies and removes the power of God and then lays claim to the very powers it has sought to obliterate in Him.

Once, when Harari was publishing a new book, , in order to get the interview, I agreed to participate in a staged event for this book's marketing campaign. It was at a school in South London, a state school in a diverse area; that's why it had been chosen for the kind of promo dressed as altruism schtick with which anyone studying the advance of neo-liberal totalitarianism will be familiar. The kids were aged between eleven and sixteen. There in the anodyne sports hall with the assembly filed in obedient rows and uniforms, Harari smilingly announced, as if it were as inevitable as falling rain or IBS, that the children there had better "learn to code," as the future belonged to automation and AI. Had I done my job and read his book I would've known what was coming but I hadn't, focusing instead on what to wear for the interview (a Dior sweater that was actually very itchy and I never wore again, even though it looked terrific: black and white, a bit gothic but stylish, certainly better than the drab uniform of the kids and Harari's gender-neutral standard, dystopian attire), and I was ambushed by this blithe Orwellianism.

I interjected, at first curious but eventually furious. "These kids don't need to submit to AI, they could dedicate their lives to overthrowing the system," I said, mostly just quoting lyrics from Pink Floyd's "The Wall," but careful to avoid the surely deliberate double-negative: "We don't need no education." We were, after all, in a school, a diverse school that I later learned is routinely used for propaganda of the type I was unwittingly participating in. They had a picture of Tony Blair on the wall. ("All in all, he's just another pr*ck on the wall.") As my Dollar-Store Che Guevara rhetoric amped up a notch, a few nervous looks were exchanged. By the time I got to inciting an "I'm Spartacus" style show of solidarity, the PR folks from Penguin Publishing gestured that the

Deputy Headmaster ought to intervene. I, emboldened by their discomfort, began to work through the gears. I turned to the dormant congregation, who at the time I hoped regarded me as a Robin Williams in Dead-Poet's-Society-type tonic, but based on my own recollections of school, they were likely just politely waiting for breaktime and their next opportunity to huff glue. Or whatever kids do these days—fentanyl? Only Fans? Only Fentanyl? The mind boggles. My tirade grew more passionate: "You must fight, you can change the world, you don't need to be enslaved, you can resist, rebel, revolt. . . . You do need no education . . ." I petered out while absolutely no one recited, "Oh Captain, my captain" or "I'm Spartacus" or offered dreary harmonies on "not needing no thought control."

Now, from my new vantage point as a servant of Christ, I recognize that my fiery incantations would just have led those kids down a hopeless path of false idolatry: sexy, godless rebellion. My point is that I got to witness, firsthand, the enthusiastic and presumptuous application of the ideas that many criticize Harari for in the most fascinating and germane environment: a school, a state school, an exemplary globalist factory farm for the next serf class, the AI slaves of the next generation being given the prompts and tools to make what they may one day regard as a personal choice they made to "learn to code." I saw cozy, soft propaganda gently indoctrinating kids, while they ought to have still been reposing in parenthetical comfort. Christ instructs that we need to return to the innocence of childhood. To attain the transcendent, we must repudiate worldliness. The Luciferian system similarly demands the innocence of children and craves our dependency, knowing we cannot serve two masters.

> "And he said: 'Truly I tell you, unless you change and become like little children, you will never enter the kingdom of heaven.'" Matthew 18:3

> "Truly I tell you, anyone who will not receive the kingdom of God like a little child will never enter it.'" Luke 18:17

Becoming a child before a God that loves you is a scary proposition for a new Christian and not easy if, like me, you've been marinated and steeped in the world's cloyingly toxic and saccharin fugue. But the alternative is to unconsciously present yourself as a child at the altar of the prince of this world, Satan. And whilst the slow tendrils of red tape and asphyxiating soma may make the impending boot imperceptible, it is coming. They want to stamp on your face forever.

I'm not suggesting that Yuval Noah Harari is evil, by the way, or anything other than a nice man and a good writer. I am saying that his books and theories are convenient to and exploitable by a set of interests that benefit from our breezy capitulation to what Harari frames as globalism's inevitable domination.

During the pandemic, it appeared to me that this model of total domination was being obscenely piloted. How faithful would the newly corralled global congregation be under explicit and restrictive new regulation? Would we "Trust the science"? Would we be willing to submit to the supreme authority of the state?

Generally, the answer was yes. Seventy percent of the global population took at least one Covid shot and were willing in a near instant to rebrand pharmaceutical giants as impeccable and reliable partners in a "health crisis," despite what we learned about their practices and methods during the opioid travesty (727,000

US deaths, $573 million paid out in compensation to victims, after a deceptive and expensive marketing strategy caused these deaths). Yet, due to the very technology that might facilitate total global domination, there was some effective pushback. Certainly, a lot more effective than that bloody vaccine.

In Proverbs, we hear how obedient in faith to our Lord we must be. This submission is advised that we may know the peace that comes from yielding to Him:

> "Trust in the LORD with all your heart and lean not on your own understanding; in all your ways submit to him, and he will make your paths straight". Proverbs 3:5–6

The state wants precisely this degree of submission and compliance, a perverse and counterfeit version of God's grace. Satan, using institutions of human power, conducts the diabolical and parodic inversion of grace, disgrace. The verse that brings home for me the powerful but curiously neglected Christian assertion that evil has captured the world is Ephesians 6:12:

> "For our struggle is not against flesh and blood, but against the rulers, against the authorities, against the powers of this dark world and against the spiritual forces of evil in the heavenly realms."

Even our own potent carnality and our plainly powerful Earthly enemies are nothing compared to the actual power that we must oppose. The power that, in fact, controls these apparently human systems.

Otherworldly dark entities are engaged in a battle for your

eternal soul, which must be first enchanted by the forces of the evil one that it may be damned.

Having quite casually, almost as an aside, announced that the devil is in charge of the world and that to survive it one (especially someone with a nonnegotiable need for connection with the divine) must induce a "spiritual experience," Jung's letter to Bill W concludes:

"'Alcohol' in Latin is 'spiritus,' and you use the same word for the highest religious experience as well as for the most depraving poison. The helpful formula therefore is: spiritus contra spiritum."

In observing this inextricable connection between addiction and the need for religion, Jung not only inspired Alcoholics Anonymous but he did something that may be even more important: He identified that in the tension between a world captured by the devil and our inherent need for a relationship with our Creator lies the battleground upon which spiritual warfare is being fought. Will you submit to worldliness and therefore ultimately to evil or will you repent and turn in Faith away from the world and towards your Creator? The Old Testament is the tale of God's people's relentless failure to obey and their consequent need for atonement. The Gospels describe how that atonement was achieved: through the birth, life, death, and resurrection of Christ. The rest of the New Testament expounds on why we must accept His sacrifice. And this book explains why should do it, right now. Not that I'm suggesting this book is a sequel to the Bible; "Bible 2"—that would be grandiose, even for me. Nevertheless, this is Day 2, and we have separated the "dark" from the "light."

The light is in the "prima materia" of your reality, your consciousness. It is in the beauty of God's creation, as you experience it. Darkness is separate from it. The world is ruled by evil entities through human institutions, whether those institutions are political or cultural. Economic or philanthropic. International or domestic. Or even anatomical and neurological: our flesh and our thoughts. Navigating the vicissitudes of the ever-varying, all-attractive, spellbinding stimulants produced by and delivered through these conduits is hard. Too hard for us. Whether we are addicts captured by chemical dependency or non-addicts attached to the myriad, multivalent viscosity of a world that wants us in its dark web, we need help. And help is here. The difficult thing for me, and maybe for you, is that we only become willing to receive the help we truly need when we are deep within the darkness.

I have an extant trial in the UK which means I cannot write anything that will prejudice the proceedings—I believe that justice is real, because I believe Jesus is real and although I believe that all human institutions, especially the ones that demonstrate the most pomp and flair, are fallen, I believe Christ can work through that. I believe he always has. I also want you to understand what it's like to be famous and wealthy and how strange, stimulating, and exciting it is to get access to easy sex when you're still a mixed-up kid. Unless you have been there, there is really no way you can know how extraordinary it is, but it is a moral problem that maps onto the culture more widely. For example, get this: Porn Hub receives more daily traffic than Netflix, TikTok, Pinterest, and Instagram combined. Masturbating over illicit material is endemic, harmful, and not being discussed with the appropriate urgency and wisdom. So, the culture at large is unduly fixated on sex. The devil uses sex as a snare—the Epstein files are as good an example as we are likely to get as to how temptation and sin are used to control even the most powerful, or seemingly most powerful people on earth. From the highest to the lowest, from elite circles of world leaders and billionaires down to immigrant Pakistani cab drivers, from inconceivably lavish parties on private islands attended by the most admired people on Earth to lowly, lonely rooms with screen lit onanists fretfully squirming in their own pixelated filth, sexual sin is everywhere. It's not a coincidence. As our friends in crypto currency are wont to say, "It's not a bug, it's a feature."

I have a different story to tell when it comes to sex, one of deprivation as a sad tubby boy, desperation as a young man, and depravity, by Bible standards, as an adult. I lived in denial of sex like many young men, then all of a sudden could have all the sex I wanted. It was like a fairy tale in its own warped way; rags to riches. What I didn't know then but I do know now is that what I was taught were riches were the filthiest rags of all.

In adolescence I was, like most teenagers, fascinated by sex and, also like most teenagers, given no clear instruction as to how these feelings ought be marshalled. It was not explained that sex has two applications; one, of course, procreation and the other, an expression of love within marriage. I saw sex in the same paradoxical way that most people do within our neo-pagan and individualistic culture. That sex is simultaneously "no big deal" and yet the most important thing there is.

I was an insecure kid that blossomed, as they say, into a pretty attractive teenager and found it comparatively easy to attract mates. I'm not talking captain-of-the-football-team levels here, but girls kinda liked me. I'm a good talker and can make people laugh. Nothing prepared me for the velocity and power of fame, though. It was kind of like a precautionary modern folk tale where to scare a juvenile Marlboro-chuffing punk straight they are confronted with a whole pack, escorted to a broom closet, and told not to come out till they're all smoked.

When you are famous, the process of seducing sexual partners is collapsed and inverted. Everywhere you go women are excited to see you. They approach you, flirt with you, touch you. It is overwhelming but you quickly adapt. If, like me, you are a live performer, there are screaming girls in the audience, literally throwing panties at you, asking you to sign their boobs, offering threesomes, freely offering instant intimacy in urgent and unsavory spaces—it is astonishing, but you quickly adapt.

I had sex with multiple women, often at the same time, most days, for years. It was normal to have three-ways and four-ways and for women who had not met prior, to fold into one flesh in my bed. It happened every day.

Here are a few occasions that stand out that will help you understand the levels of excess, the sheer abundance and the implausibility, the pointlessness, of coercion (if you own an orchard, you don't steal apples), as well as the hollow sadness that is an inevitable accompaniment to all forms of addiction and sin.

After a transatlantic flight from LA, I invited the whole female flight crew back to my house. They came. They drank and we all messed around. Some of them were married, or in relationships. Their uniforms were strewn across my floor. It seemed cool, like *Catch Me if You Can* or *Shampoo*, like I was lovable because they wanted me. I got my sense of self-worth from their attraction to me. I guess I remember it because it was cinematic; the flight continued way beyond LAX to Heathrow, and it ended in my bed. I felt like an alchemist, I could create ecstasy out of mundanity. When I would tell my male friends these stories, especially older married ones, I felt so valuable and impressive. Now I see these things very differently.

After a show at the Brixton Academy, the female cast of a popular reality TV show tumbled out of the after-party and poured into my hot tub with no more fanfare or fuss than I once would have tipped the contents of an instant soup into a mug. There were at least five of them, a couple of them were sisters. As if some dormant part of me, alive only in Christ, already knew the man I would become, the challenges and trials I would face, and the significant fact that I myself would one day be a father to daughters, the apparent mad and hedonic glamor was haunted by something I couldn't understand. As these beautiful young women kissed me and each other and craned over my body, I saw myself dead, I felt like I was a roadside corpse being picked over by vultures. I felt like an iron and inanimate ride at a fiendish amusement park, detached, imploding. It was still a great story to tell my friends, but I felt the hollow truth in my belly when I recounted the tale as surely as if it were a gnawing beak.

In Sydney, Australia, after a party that was thrown for me at a hotel with a rooftop pool, the kind of glory that only a foolish and fallen ego would thirst after, I quickly left with a couple of women who, once back at my place, didn't want to have sex; they changed their minds. This happened sometimes. There followed a kind of fatigued dispute—from my perspective, a line of willing participants coiled around the block. I with the automatic and hopeless bored compulsion that probably only addicts know returned to my phone and group texts like Sisyphus to his boulder. That's what always happened if a woman changed her mind. She'd leave, and I'd invite others. I am aghast to recount it, but human beings and their special, unique, and divine value would, to me, at times like that, be as interchangeable as fast-food drive thru's. If McDonald's is closed, we go to KFC. You don't take a hatchet to Ronald McDonald unless you're a sicko, I suppose. It's not my thing, it never has been. Now we know that across our culture, whether its British Pakastani "Rape Gangs" or the elites of world power, rape and sexual abuse are routine.

I want to be wanted, adored, and lost in worship, me of them, them of me. We know that some men enjoy domination, exploitation, humiliation. Not me; the essence that I now know I was trying to access is worship. Unity. Connection. In short, love.

I now realize that you can only achieve that intimacy through Christ.

Back then, I dedicated myself to becoming desirable and it worked. There were some occasions, not as many as I dreamed, where I felt like Jagger, in a semi-Moroccan robe, something that flowed, while women that loved me and one another cavorted and fornicated and it seemed like sin was working. Like hedonism and Sex Magick and shamanism and new paganism and me as a Jim-Morrison-sex-priest would all work out. But even before the retro-engineered allegations, I knew that it was not right, that it was outside of a covenant that I didn't know but could somehow intuit.

But if you have never known what it's like—and unless you are an appealing, famous man, you probably don't—it is impossible to imagine the sacred and rare treasure of sex recast as an easily available commodity, as consumable and accessible as Coca Cola. I'd read about this way of life in other famous men's biographies, but I've also read about space travel and I'm guessing from what I've read there is some distance from the ontological mind fuck of walking on the moon. To have sex with shopkeepers and realtors and masseuses and waitresses and photographers and doctors and lawyers and movie stars, with pop stars and TV execs and journalists, it does something to you, and it isn't good, it inures you, it breaks you, it desensitizes you. It will damage you as a person and hurt other people for sure. But the last thing it will make you do is force people to have sex if they don't want to. In the book of James it says, "We consider it pure joy when we face trials of any kind," and this is the verse that my wife Laura put on the painting of a magnolia she made and tucked into my Bible as I travelled from Florida to the UK to enter my "Not guilty" plea to these charges for alleged events between 1999 and 2007, when I was a different man in many ways but not the man they claim.

Two kids in, and at the twenty-six-week scan of kid number three, and I can barely be bothered to train my eyes on the screen. Like the disciples who become in the presence of Our Lord, insatiable miracle junkies, no sooner has he turned water into wine and they are jonesing for a walk across the Sea of Galilee. A few days later they are clucking for Him to feed the five thousand. That soon wears off and they rattle like mad for a transfiguration or a healed leper. It seems ridiculous that they're never satisfied till I consider my own incessant demand for and ingratitude towards the miraculous. Back in the clinic the beeps, the foggy, grainy, submarine imagery, the "If you squint you can see it" feet and features. Especially at the fag-end of the pandemic. When your marriage ain't going great, and you're decades into your life as an addict in recovery, a father and online content creator, daily proselytizing on the conspiracies of the day. Like, "The function of government is to transfer public money into private interests" (Julian Assange). Or "When interests converge no conspiracy is necessary" (George Carlin) and trying to say it in fresh new ways and wondering why trying to provide funny content while "Speaking truth to power" isn't remotely fulfilling anymore. In fact, I was just about to take my daughters to the park; they were rattling and spiking around the room tearing off blue paper towels, trying to touch the gel on Laura's belly. I'd already blown up a rubber glove like an udder and was now fresh out of ideas. This scan was a formality, the doctor's clinic as much inclined towards beauty as interventional medicine. I once had some "love-handle" fat frozen off in an anti-chamber there. I'm pretty embarrassed about it, but there you are. In the room adjacent to the beeps and blue towels and five-fingered tiny Hindenburg, was a merchandise room, an Aladdin's cave of senseless baubles made to be adorned with images snatched from straightforward scans: mugs with radiant faces of golden in-utero angels, cuddly little rabbits bearing a frame to hold same, keyrings and plates and all sorts of opportunistic trinkets ordained with grandma in mind, landfill in waiting but certainly a good way to stiff arm a rabid nana who might otherwise demand actual access to your family. This I mention only to say that the scan was, in my mind at least, a hemmed-in thing, a theme park, a safe trot through the stations of pregnancy with no inchoate need to confront the dreadful fragility of life. I may as well have lit a fag or cracked open a can as I sighed and sidled my way towards the door, my bored daughters almost an excuse for my own departure. My hand and my eyes were on the handle when the lady with the transducer almost hiccupped my name. "Russell." She didn't call me "Mister Brand" but she may as well have done because the tone was unmistakable. A certain timber or cadence of some dark melody, a reminder then for tunes to make sense at all there must be some recipient, a partner, for there to be meaning there must be someone to perceive it.

I knew from this incursive word, downward turned, halting but not faltering that some new thread was being spun, and I ushered forth the sisters out of the range of this new foe and soberly returned, this time seated, not pacing.

The sonographer pointed at a barely discernible thing but I wasn't looking at the monitor; I wasn't even looking at her face or my wife's. I was looking into the certain past from whence I'd been long-primed. I knew this day would come. "You see this movement here?" I couldn't. "This is blood exiting from (I think she said) the right ventricle chamber." (I think it was ventricle, it was a school word, a science word, not a good word, not a keyring word) "it should be coming out from here. . . ."

But I'm no longer in the room, I'm in the new but familiar purgatorial gloom, that spiraling, imploding fold, that twilight behind childhood curtains when there's still the chuckling requiem of play out on the street, the hospital waiting rooms where unqualified relatives would pat my shoulder while my Mum adjusted a wig. Dead dogs, an unwelcome hand between my legs, the sharp splat of ejaculate on the cistern, the breach and tear of shielded time, the unwelcome hand in no man's land, in the land with no man.

I don't let her finish. I try to stab back at time. "Is this ever going to be nothing again?" is the question that I ask, that best surmises all that I want to convey to this woman who I blame.

"No."

Maybe, I was thinking, *I could get a better and more expensive obstetric sonographer or a better machine, one for celebrities' babies, or one for men who have pulled themselves up by their bootstraps and overcome addiction and "all the odds." Maybe I can think or write or fuck or fight my way out of this.* But no.

She's already said, "No."

It's never going to be nothing again. Pretty soon I'm out the room, I suppose the gel on the belly must've been wiped off with the blue towels and the glove balloon deflated. Pretty soon we're in another room, my wife and me. The room where I had fat frozen off my lower back, it's just cells after all; I'm not sure it even worked. The stupid vain room for stupid vain procedures for stupid vain people. In vain, the fat is still there. Too quickly I am saying, "I'm not going to Great Ormond Street, Lor', I'm not dealing with all the pipes and masks and wires and tubes." Especially the tubes. And now we are confronted, she and I, she and me, we. We are confronted. We are two kids deep and we are being given new direction, sharp correction, and I do not want it. Then we are in a playground and the kids are carrying on. Small town, England, climbing frame, swing, crisp packet, sick. A sign denoting some tedious history of the town. "Someone did something here once." Who cares?

Room after room now, bigger hospitals, more expensive, more letters after more names. Waiting rooms, Latin and Greek like you wouldn't believe; pediatric cardiologist, cardio-pediatric ologist obstetric in utero pedio hat trick. No keyrings though. No keyrings now.

This guy actually sighs as he does the scan. This pedio-cardio-utero bloke, he actually sighs and shakes his head. He stops short of sucking his teeth like a mechanic and saying, "I Dunno mate, it's gonna cost ya..." but it will, and it did. He asks if we want to know the sex of the baby. With the last two we wanted the surprise but now we've had enough in surprises. He scans and sighs and squints a bit then says, "It's a boy. You're having a son."

Was that . . . Just . . . a . . . tiny . . . glimpse . . . of . . . something

. . . there . . . Lord? Was it hope? Was it beauty? Was it peace beyond understanding? Is it the Kingdom, my Lord?

Now back to the purgatorial drag in another gloom room. I can sense the car park out the window behind him even though we are high up. Our daughters were born here.

"We initially thought it was transposition of the arteries . . ."

Why do they always say "we"? I'll tell you why, it's for authority and validation;

"You're not just talking to me, you're talking to a whole tradition and body of empirical evidence, you're talking to Galileo and Copernicus and Stephen Hawking and Marie Curie (better put a woman in) and Einstein. But not Bruno Giordino who mystically foresaw multiverses, or Einstein when he says, "God does not play dice." Or presumably, Anthony Fauci when he said, "I am science," which is so demagogic and egotistical that it's more like something Rick James would say if he were running the CDC. Which he'd probably be better at than Fauci and we'd almost certainly get some reliable data on cocaine.

"From the scan we now think it's Tetralogy of Fallot . . ." Who is this *we*? Is it to have plausible deniability if something goes wrong, more wrong?

"Which is four combined heart conditions . . ."

For the price of one?

"The four components are one: Ventricular Septal Defect , a hole between the heart's two lower pumping chambers."

Okay.

"Two: Pulmonary Stenosis; a narrowing of the pulmonary valve and the artery leading to the lungs."

Right.

"Three: Right Ventricular Hypertrophy, a thickening of the

muscular wall of the lower right chamber, caused by the heart working too hard. And four: Overriding Aorta, the body's main artery is misplaced, sitting over the hole in the heart instead of above the left ventricle."

"But . . . otherwise, okay?"

"Well . . ."

Uh oh.

"Babies with Tetralogy of Fallot have a significant chance of also having another congenital defect, with estimates generally falling in the twenty to twenty-five percent range."

I like those odds, keep talking.

"Firstly. DiGeorge syndrome (22q11.2 deletion syndrome): Is one of the most frequent genetic conditions linked with TOF. Around fifteen percent of all individuals with TOF also have DiGeorge syndrome. The risk increases further, to nearly fifty percent, for those with a specific variation called pulmonary atresia with major aorto-pulmonary collateral arteries."

Cool.

"Secondly, Down syndrome . . ."

Yeah, I've heard of that one.

"Yes, we also call it Trisomy 21: This is another common genetic disorder seen in babies with TOF, accounting for roughly seven percent of cases."

I'm not good at math.

"Other less common syndromes also linked to TOF include Alagille syndrome, CHARGE syndrome, and VACTERL association."

Got it.

"It is important to note that about seventy-five to eighty percent of TOF cases occur without any known associated syndrome or chromosomal abnormality. In these instances, the heart defect is considered an isolated condition."

Thanks. "Do you validate parking?"

"No. We do that downstairs . . ."

We?

"Actually, it's a machine."

I have never received a more severe correction in my life than I did when I learned of my son's congenital heart condition. "I knew this would happen," I said in a meeting with men in recovery in my bunker, the same garage that the studio is in. My life was heading in one direction, and I thought I was in control. In one moment, everything changed, a stranger said my name, and nothing was ever the same.

Day Two: *Hope*

> God spoke: "Sky! In the middle of the waters; separate water from water!"
>
> God made sky. He separated the water under sky from the water above sky.
>
> And there it was: he named sky the Heavens; It was evening, it was morning— Day Two.
>
> Genesis 1:6 The Message

Sky is an expanse of hope, new horizons, new realms. Some water flows, some water, vapor, is suspended in air. God makes distinction and righteous separation. Are you ready to separate from the person you were before Christ? Dare you hope that you might be saved?

Please Consider that in this crisis of your dead life is a chance, a window, a thread, that leads to new life.

Are you willing to envisage a Christ that hasn't come to you via the culture (South Park Jesus, blonde Jesus) or a reductive and inarticulate church (pious, effete Jesus)?

You know so many phony Jesuses (what's the plural for fake Jesuses? Jesi?) that you cannot locate the Real Christ. Are you willing to consider the weirdly mythic, near orgasmic, glitchy, mind-melting possibility that if you had been alive in Galilee in the year zero you could've seen God walking around in flesh?

Are you (Russell?! Say your name here) willing to, with a fresh, new mind, ask "Jesus, are you Real?"

Can you see the tomb?

Easter morning, the stone rolled aside, the Christ, eerily and uncannily only part recognizable to his intimate disciples, emerging with a new body, wounded hands, an angel by the tomb. This is an overwhelming supernatural truth and it relates, strangely, to me and you. He did it for me and you.

For a person who believes in the culture, which amounts to worshipping yourself in a seemingly individually curated form, your likes, dislikes, petty wants and needs, it's very hard to open anew to the possibility of the unseen world. But through this image, this moment, the resurrection, life after crucifixion, this is what you must do.

I didn't believe I ever could but now I do, sometimes it goes out of focus, if I am afraid or tired or in desire but it has become, HE has become the foundation of my life, the Rock. *What is your rock*? Please answer below.

What is your life based on?

Is it family?

Is it work?

Whatever it is, it is "that thing" in relationship to you, obviously. But you have admitted on day one your fallibility and hopelessness. We cannot anchor our own lives.

Here we must open to hope in Him. To stop saying "no," to begin to say "I don't know," then, "I invite You in, Lord."

Can you?

You have honestly admitted that your life alone is finished.

Remember?

You did it yesterday.

If you're anything like me, and fundamentally you are, you are already renegotiating with yourself.

"I'm alright."

"It wasn't that bad."

"Maybe if I get a new partner/sex-person/job/dog/shoe?"

I'm starting to see that no object, idol, aim can ever work for me. Can you? Not when the opponent is death, racing down the track, pummeling down the tunnel.

"Maybe if I have sex with a dog in a shoe, then everything will be okay?"

I can save you, based on personal experience of at least twenty-five to thirty years, by telling you it won't be alright.

If money made it okay, I would never have found Him.

If sex had or drugs had, or fame or even pantheism and family, I would never have found Him.

If I hadn't been through, well, literally everything in this book, which you've read over a quarter of and by tomorrow over half, I wouldn't have found Him.

I've been through a lot. Whether you like me or not, you'd have to give me that.

And I am transformed. Still broken, still a sinner, still wounded but saved. I trust Him. Like I tried to trust me. This works.

I know and I hope you do too that He makes sense of suffering through His sacrifice and forgiveness.

That nothing short of God's love will save you from this living death you're distracting yourself from. I will admit that I've never *had sex with a dog in a shoe*, so maybe that's another potential answer?

The way things are going I'll probably be charged with that by the time the book's out.

Even that don't matter because God is Real.

Look at your list from yesterday. Go on, you poor sod. Right, it's a sorry state of affairs, you've been trying to wring God's glory out of this filthy rag of a material world—not that God's creation isn't beautiful, it is, because it's infused with His love. But you can't, as you know, from yesterday, distill or otherwise extract pleasure from this creation apart from our Creator.

If that were possible, you wouldn't be reading this book and I wouldn't have written it.

For a few minutes, reflect on someone you know has found God.

If you can't think of anyone, there's me, Thomas Aquinas and quite a few Saints, some saints in waiting move among us and we should, as the old hymn says, want to be in that number, plus probably at least one of your grandparents. Don't be thinking of religious people that have been proven assholes—like someone that's abused you when you were a kid—that's a common trick to prevent progress.

I would like you to imagine the instances on your previous list improving, yet I want to say that material guarantees are not what the spiritual life is about.

This world is fleeting and "All is vanity."

But through it, even the most painful things, we can glimpse Him. Thomas Merton (saint, priest, previously Buddhist) said "sacrifice needn't include suffering." This is pretty mind-blowing to a Christian because the ultimate image and axis at the center of reality is God on the cross, but even the word paradox suggests a cross.

Merton means that this event has reset reality, and you now have a choice as to whether to join it.

You can turn away from your brokenness and toward Him.

He suffered for us. The apparent contradiction is that suffering is, of course the result of attachment, attachment is temporary (in/of time), and sacrifice is a portal, a door, a way, a vine through which you can (if you don't love your life) travel to freedom.

If you have relinquished your life (and you haven't yet, neither have I, neither did Saint Paul entirely, at points) you would access this Power without suffering.

So:

Read the Bible.

I started with Acts in The Message, because that's what "Father," now Bishop, Dave Bull told me to do. It worked.

I kept thinking, "This happened." This is the best we can get, here on this bandwidth, with these limits and these advantages (epistemological frailty, free will), "These people, His first followers, are like me."

Then I read *The Bible in One Year* by Nicky Gumbel and Pippa Gumbel.

He is in there. I mean Jesus, not Nicky.

Then I noticed new Christians. Clever, kind, cool. I'd never seen them before. Although they must've been, most of them, at first were older than me. Some of them by centuries. Many of them are cleverer than me.

If you think you personally have resolved or seen something that eluded C. S. Lewis, I'd like to take you for coffee and have you explain it to me.

Don't be embarrassed; you probably had Christianity demonstrated to you by idiots.

It's not about them, or you. Or, *gulp*, even me.

It's about Jesus Christ the Son of the Living God, born of the Virgin, died on the cross to absolve our sin, rose again on the third day, ascended into heaven.

I know that's what they say, and how remote it can seem.

Consider watching and reading Father Mike Schmitz, Ruth Burrows . . . I mean there are so many beautiful, light, or intense and strange Christians. There's someone for everyone. He is infinitely creative.

How else would He have dreamed up J John (look him up)?

I could never have conceived of such a lovely, kind, clever, brilliant, unusual, unearthly man.

Hope is all you need. I have it and I struggle to believe you are more hopeless than me.

The Third Day: Faith

Let there be dry land

"Dear Jesus, please get me out... If you only keep me from being killed I'll do anything you say."

Ernest Hemingway

"Fear not, for I have redeemed you; I have called you by name, you are mine."

Isiah 43:1

Can we have an identity beyond the pain and shame inflicted by the world? Can we escape our slavery to sin? To self?

> "The people remained at a distance, while Moses approached the thick darkness where God was." Exodus 20:21

Immediately after the instructions for survival are issued—the ten commandments—the Israelites freak out. The noise of trumpets and celestial disruption unsettle them, and they turn to their leader and mediator Moses for intercessional support. May I say that as someone who has only just read the Bible for the first time, I'm pretty astonished by the disobedience of this little crowd; they never miss an opportunity to play up, disobey, complain, get distracted. Yahweh, far from being a vindictive and punishing God, is as far as I can see breathtakingly patient. In particular, during the Exodus "wilderness years," the Israelites are crying out for a good smiting. The noncompliance and ingratitude just around the manna issue would be enough for most omnipotent deities to consider letting the walls of the Red Sea close in and wipe them out. To approach God, Moses must leave the crowd and enter a "thick darkness." My own intimacy with our Lord has had precisely this flavor. To be near God I have had to leave everyone else behind and enter into a thick darkness. Unlike most of us, certainly unlike me, Moses appears to have (at least once activated by mission) a great willingness to collapse his own identity in order to meet God. We are made in God's image, the hallmark of this image is the face—the face, incidentally, is what Orwell's figurative tyrannical boot desecrates in his metaphor for a totalitarian future. Moses covers his face, lies face down, and later exclusively reveals his face to God. In order to meet God, I had to leave the crowd behind, and I had to enter a thick darkness, alone.

"Everything's a burning bush," snarled Daniel. This vet amputee, stomping through D.C., made his declaration from nowhere, but it makes more sense to me every day.

I was in D.C. for the Inauguration of Trump, attending one or two events, surrendered really to the unfurling path, simply trying to say yes to the day, trying to trust that the Lord would take me where he wants me. Attempting not to cling or grind or push at life, trying not to wrest satisfaction out of this world. No longer gathering approval or applause or frottaging after comfort. No longer objectifying women sexually or men as receptacles of opportunity or power. So, I accepted the invitation to attend a MAHA ball (Make America Healthy Again), I accepted the ride in Ajay's plane (my beloved friend Ajay Gupta), I accepted the Bible Museum's offer to let me sleep in their museum (like *Night at the Museum*, insane). I accepted a ride from some guys at the Washington airport who happened to be heading to an event at the Bible Museum. It was cold in D.C. and a phalanx of private planes flanked the runway in the frost like iron swans at an asphalt trough. I took a ride with the tuxedoed men who I'd never seen before and I've never seen again. I listened to their private calls in the blue light. I swallowed down doubt. We arrived at the Bible Museum, vast, magnificent. I went to my room that overlooked the illuminated Capitol, and I peeked and pondered in the creepy cold. I accepted the invitation to attend a swanky event downstairs. D.C. is Rome. Time trapped in monuments, a monument is time, a moment captured and trapped. There he is: Lincoln, vast sedentary patriarch. There he is: Jefferson in silent declaration, but where is Ozymandias? Eaten by sand and by untrapped time. Since January 6, the symbol of the Capitol must now, like so many icons, fragment its meaning for an endlessly divided culture. One marvels at the ire of the pearl-clutching swine that genuflect before the D.C. gods; "They stormed the Capitol?! That's where we conduct our vile hypocrisy!" "They could've knocked over a lobbyist!" "What if a corrupt congressman had been taking a bribe? Or molesting a child and had been jostled by that filthy mob? "Do you think it's easy to traffic kids in D.C. with all this Epstein controversy going on?!" There is, I understand, a fresco of George Washington ascending, Christ-like into heaven, which is as clear an example of the nation usurping religion as supreme authority as we're going to get. But I'm English and I can never really appreciate American patriotism. My love of my nation will always include a deep loathing for almost all the icons of its power. The monarchy, especially post-Elizabeth the Second, has the shelf life of air miles accrued on Lolita Air, Epstein's jet. Keir Starmer seems to have been divinely designed to undermine the office of Prime Minister. If Washington is depicted as an American Enoch (who ascended, it surely can't be an American Jesus, that's actual Jesus!) then Trump as an American mystic is doable. The prophet America conjured from a fraught but mutual mythic imagination. Of course, this media-steeped and slick age would call, in the end, for a viciously effective media operator. Of course, after Clinton, Blair, and Obama and in their unctuous wake we'd obviously need a kind of uber, yet anti-president with sarcastic hair and a PhD in wisecrackery and intuitive social media expertise. Of course, an American mystic, the apotheosis of the American dream, has his own name on towers and planes and bath soap and literally eats McDonald's and drinks Coke. Somehow our latter-day meta, simulation culture demanded him, brought him forth. There's no question that he is better than the alternative. If this peace deal, or tariff or whatever we are clinging to now holds till publication, it'll certainly be difficult to argue.

I attend the inauguration eve event in the spooky bustle of the sparse night and reckon you can't mend America here. Deep tides move beneath the stones and columns. More tuxedos, fine dresses, hundreds of thousands of dollars of flowers, and a dog that has more online followers than I do. It was wearing a sweater and, I think, though I struggle to see how this can be right, that it was an expert in bitcoin. Anyway, I had to crouch down to have my photo with it. In more ways than one.

Thankfully, the ambiguity was shattered by Shilo Harris, a veteran in attendance whose service cost him his face, like Moses, but gave him a new one, like Moses. Amidst the frocks and the flowers and somewhere beyond the crypto dog I see him, and he invites me to come to an event the next day for Help a Hero, a charity that builds and adapts homes for war veterans that well, you know, have lost a limb or become in some other way impaired through service. I want you to know that I didn't willfully go to Washington, I went because it seemed like I was supposed to; I followed a chain of invitations. I want you to understand that I am trying to live in Christ, and while the best examples of living in Him will always include heroic sacrifice, those pinnacle demonstrations of Christlike living are rare, and it is by them that saints are made. Achieving a state of active surrender through faith is a less noble demonstration but it marks for me a significant departure from my normal fraught devotion to fretful and grasping self-will. I'm not claiming that my attending events connected to the inauguration has any intrinsic value, just that I am living in a state of openness that is uncustomary and is producing unusual results. And while the pageantry of power that coronations and inaugurations muster seems macabre to me, in surrender I was led into encounters that I would never have sought through my own volition. I spent the night at the museum. It's as preposterous as you would imagine and involves a nocturnal tour and the torch-lit study of a second-century mosaic floor known as the

"Megiddo mosaic," with Mattheus from the museum and a few refugees from the 1775 event that I'd been briefly attending after an invite from the limo men. If anyone should be keen to evacuate the patriotic and elegantly jingoistic 1775 event, given the significance of that date, it should be me, the lone Englishman, I would be entitled to gallop out like Paul Revere. Yep, I'm learning.

The mosaic was discovered in 2005 during an archaeological excavation beneath a maximum-security prison in Israel. The Israeli prisoners themselves participated in the excavation and the mythic intensity of condemned men unearthing from beneath the penitentiary dirt an artifact that includes the inscription, "God Jesus Christ" is so dense with the kind of ubiquitous prophetic poetry that Daniel illumined with his maxim and inevitable T-shirt slogan, "Everything's a burning bush" that it's messing with the chronology of this chapter. I met him the next morning after taking up Shilo's invitation and sleeping in a suite in the Bible Museum called "Galilee" and eating a gifted basket of toffee popcorn for breakfast: "I eat gifted toffee popcorn like you for breakfast." I can be a vagrant anywhere, even in a complimentary executive suite in a beautiful museum, snacking on a gift basket, I feel the edges of the vagabond life still ghosting quietly by.

"The gutter, him dun want me everywhere I be, even when in luxury he hunts and bothers me."

You know the hungry gutter, if you've ever been poor and down, if you've ever been junky. You feel its grimy fingers slide past sybaritic defenses. I can turn a five-star hotel room into Gollum's Grotto just by brushing my teeth in it. And my kids drop three social classes as soon as my wife moves fifty yards away. The gutter is a greedy foe, I tell thee.

I arrived late at the Help a Hero, or Home a Hero or Help Home a Hero event, I don't recall the exact name; I know they prioritized alliteration over memorability, and as soon as I entered the downstairs convention room at the mid-range hotel venue, I started to feel better. It was only half full, or half empty (you decide!) and the chairs were lined up like crooked teeth, like the event had been shuffling along for few hours. There was a stage and a screen and the half-filled helium balloon hover of a wrung-out presentation. I was given a mic and steered towards the stage and it's not until I faced out that I saw where I was. Veterans are young now, like policemen. Like footballers or even football managers. But veterans especially were old if you're English (I'm English). They have flat caps and brown coats and bald heads and medals and on Poppy Day they stand disheveled, proud, or they hunch or are pushed in wheelchairs down Whitehall towards The Cenotaph to lay poppy wreaths where the obelisk hits the ground, where the rubber meets the road. But now these veterans are young, like doe-eyed young, fit and vee-shaped, handsome and with stubble. When I looked closer, I saw that some were missing limbs. One guy in a cowboy hat had a robot arm and a leather woven sling and wrap-around shades, like an X-man, like several X-Men; if you were writing it, you'd redistribute some of his attributes to provide flavor across the cast. Some were missing legs. Look closer and you'd see something in their eyes that's hard to describe but is connected, I think, to what those eyes have themselves looked at, like something went in, never left and can still be seen in there now.

Gary Shandling's acting coach, Roy London, said that in performance art we want to see just one moment of authenticity. This new tendency, since coming to Christ, to try to be present with Him, and surrendered to Him in each moment, generates authentic connection. I am learning how to reliably and consistently do it. Sometimes still I recoil in fear, I retract, I grip and clench with revulsion or desire, but Day 3 of *How to Become a Christian in Seven Days* (or your money back*) is about preparing to trust and surrender.

I heard, "If you went to the circus and watched a highwire artist push a wheelbarrow along the tightrope across the Big Top, you'd have faith that he'd get to the other side. But if you had trust, you'd be willing to get in the wheelbarrow." Bob D. I tumbled through this inauguration trip, pulled by a force as independent of me as gravity but as impactful on me as . . . also gravity, and it paid off here when The Lord showed up and gave me some lessons and to make sure I didn't miss them, they all came in the names of Old Testament Prophets.

I spotted him as I was taking in the room and talking out an intro. He's hard to miss, built like a Nose Tackle (I learned that term for this simile), puppyish and smooth, radiant and kind, even at thirty yards, from where you cannot see the seared-in eye pain. Meredith the great matriarch that has conceived of this cause after the loss of some beloved told me, as I had nattered, that I had to talk to Amos Benjamin. Now lately, since becoming Christian, new channels have opened, it is not an intellectual or social exercise that I am involved in, more a deep unbidden alchemy in the soil of my being, some still yet intermittent reversal of the charge, the unremittent and inward cling has been reversed by Him into a luminescent inner transmission. And the upshot of it is that I cry a lot more. I weep. I'd locked up all my Mummy's Boy tears into a cage of fame and stagnant certainty, Christ came, and the rock became water. I was addressing the vets and as best I could, entertaining the room, when I found a melody of simpatico. I saw those men, men who not long ago I'd've been a million cultural miles away from (they were pretty psyched about Trump, American patriots, warriors, war heroes) but in the flow of my communion from the stage I'd now dismounted, as their injuries I counted, I felt a strange connection. We live by faith and not by sight as we cede to His New Covenant.

Passover Feast 1992, with the Hirsch family, me and Matt on LSD sit through Barry at the table head's solemn incantations, me a high gentile, I feel, as if carried by a reddening Nile, a plague of ancient sadness. I cry and it's not entirely unpleasant, in the way that real sorrow surpasses vague and fugitive happiness. Man, I felt them Israelites that strung out high on acid Pacer night.

I had by now moved to the floor in front of the stage, to achieve a better connection, perched, one knee bent upon my chair, my other foot on the carpet as a pivot when something came over me as I noticed that inadvertently my posture mimicked a temporary amputation. And I fell through the preceding years, all the selfishness and suffering and as I gave way to the tears as Amos was approaching, I sunk down into the chair but as the ex-marine embraced me, he pulled me up to his full height and cocked his head to face me.

Seated, we talked before the group and the young man shared his testimony. The story includes such brutal loss, it's a wonder he survived it. In brief: His brother was a marine before him, signing up and training with a friend, eventually they graduated together. The friend got Amos's brother to do a tour that he was intended to do in his stead because his wife was having their baby. On this tour, Amos's brother was killed in action. Amos was himself early in his career as a Marine and his recounting of how his commanding officer conveyed the news of his brother's death was poignant and tragic. The subsequent season of rage, attempted suicide, actual suicides, and eventual redemption that followed was a lot to absorb then and too much to retell with the display of emotional competence and eloquence that Amos produced that day. Thankfully, he has since written a book about it—*Encountering Peace: Finding My Purpose Through Loss, Faith, and Resistance*—which I wholeheartedly recommend. As he completed his outstanding tale he accented, a kind of intuitive coda, that he had cause after all his trials to look up the definition of his name, and he held his composure to this point, "Amos means: able to carry." Now it was his turn to cry and as he did, I stood and, in my embrace, pulled this man of considerable size from his chair to his feet, matching and completing our encounter's opening. The members of the audience that were able to stand got to their feet and the event was concluded.

You will all, I'm sure, be familiar in one way or another with the phenomena of "chasing the night," not wanting to go home, needing one more drink, hit, adventure or flirt before conceding defeat and going to sleep. Now, while this event had been mid-morning and no one there was drinking, I still had that feeling of not wanting to go home. Me and the vets and their relatives swapped stories, theirs Vietnam, mine Dagenham, Afghanistan versus Diddy parties, Navy Seals versus meeting Seal. Purple Hearts versus, well, purple hearts. It was snowing and the chances of returning to Florida were diminishing as airports and roads closed.

Daniel marches through time and works for the charity. He

was breaking down the screens and posters, lights, etcetera that adorn such events. He, too, is a vet and carried out the teardown tasks so swiftly, expertly, and basically joyfully that it seems almost impolite to mention that he has one leg. The loss of that limb has been so plainly converted to a net gain that it doesn't seem appropriate to describe it as a disability. He has the kind of facially open, boundlessly lit presence that I've come to recognize in Christians of a certain type. A million miles from the compromises I'd projected onto people of Faith at the start of these pages. I now know a tribe of valiant and sincere, funny and reborn men and women who, through their love, not sentiment, have demonstrated Dietrich Bonhoeffer's phrase, "Your life as a Christian should make non-believers question their disbelief in God." Daniel, amidst the removal of lighting rigs and the loading of carts, now gently snarled, "Everything's a burning bush." I stare like Bear when he watches me eat steak, hopefully without the unbroken string of drool. "Moses could've seen that bush at any time." I'm still staring. "The world is incandescent with a light that does not consume it."

I almost whine, "It's not only the stark and significant moments of your life in which God is present, He is the ever-present creator, His hallmark is beyond molecular time, His miracles are perennially possible. Moses saw God then because He was ready—'Remove your shoes for you stand on Holy Ground.' We always stand upon Holy Ground, God is always present, how could he not be?" God was there then, God is here now. God is with you now. Everything is a burning bush.

And on this little inaugural jaunt in which I'd done my best to follow the flow, and not say no and be open, and to trust, the Lord had led me to these men. While our culture throbs and scratches, clutching for ever new ways to hate, to oppose, to damn, to grandstand, to invert principles as soon as its convenient, so that it becomes impossible to track which side believes in free speech or taking on corporations or protecting the poor, or ending war, or freedom or eating good food, God's people are serving the Lord, in their brokenness and in faith, imperfect but forgiven. Providing a living temple and sacrifice for our Lord, their lives turned to Him and away from the performative political debates and the futile charge that comes from unending polemics. The culture is cunning in the way that it condemns. The drummed-up loathing for the "basket of deplorables" is easily undone in a quick trip to southern Alabama (I live so far south that I have to drive north to get to The South) when you learn that the southern man with truck and gun that hunts is likely just a Christian and Republican. Capable and competent, able to hunt and fish and fix things. Among the rednecks, my greatest discovery has been that their independence and competence has been, with insidious sophistry, recast as racism and misogyny. That to generate inordinate and unending hate, people from different social groups are being unfalteringly coached in rancor. The comic Dave Smith observed that as the Occupy movement inspired by the financial crash in 2008 began to take root and, indeed, rhizomatically connect previously opposing political factions as activists from the left and right began to cooperate on the definitive issues of global corporatism, financial elitism, government collaboration and media deception. "Identity Politics" was amplified, if not concocted, to ensure that an irresoluble cultural conflict would replace the plausible and effective alliances that threatened the centralized hegemony. When I was lapping up the froth and sputum of ridiculous praise in LA, I would have obediently believed that the men of Texas, Missouri, and Louisiana were my natural enemies.

When at the MTV VMA's in 2008, I mocked the Jonas Brothers for their chastity rings. I was queasily certain that I was right about promiscuity and pleasure and the pursuit of orgasm and treasure as the whole point of my life, that indeed it was my life. Competent men that would kill and die for what they believe in were obviously terrifying to me. Now I see that the liberal state is not liberal at all; it wants to mother and smother all potency out of you, it wants to coddle you into convalescence. It doesn't want armed men organizing their own community, supporting the vulnerable through their service to Christ. It wants you to be infantilized and compromised. We all know now that the network of Deep State blackmail umbrellaed by the near synecdoche "Epstein Files" refers to the imperiled individuals, groups, and states compromised by evidence of sexually dubious or even criminal encounters. The world's most powerful people, it is supposed, are controlled by a set of interests, superficially Mossad, MI5, CIA but ultimately whatever steers these agencies, to the point that they are lackeys rather than leaders, enslaved rather than empowered. This phenomenon of control through shame is more pervasive, though, than that. The political elite, it seems, are controlled through acute conspiracy and masterful entrapment, but the modality trickles down through the hierarchal tiers of our culture like a terraced paddy field, the purported Diddy parties and Babylonic pursuits that plainly prop up the entertainment industry, all the way down to the slurry of the lowest tiers where most people who live bereft and secular lives, defaulting the easy worship of the culture's gods, watch porn and chug down caustic values without knowing they are imbibing poison. In the same way that in a century we went from making food at home from scratch to in some cases 70 percent of calories consumed being from processed food, we live in a zoo, a farm, where our food, our information, our innermost needs are being synthetically bonded to centrally controlled systems. Once we hunted and gathered and thrived on variety. Now through successive revolutions that could have granted comfort, greater control is leveraged. In the agricultural revolution man masters nature, in the industrial revolution man masters matter, in the technological revolution that's unfolding now man is mastering attention, perhaps even consciousness. But the successive revolutions metastasize and interact, we now have industrialized agriculture and agriculture enhanced by technology, to the degree that seeds are patented and instructed in obsolescence. What drives this progress? And Cui Bono? I'm not suggesting that modern farming practices haven't fed a lot of people but what I contest is that the subsidiary benefits to a population at large are the inadvertent side effect of centralizing wealth and power. Industry is outsourced to the subcontinent and will soon be automated.

Farmers across the world are being bankrupted and capsized by top-down edicts of control. There will be a requirement for a serf class of some description, a managerial, laptop class and supervision for unblocking sewers but the truth is that the peasant class that became the labor class that became the service industry class have nearly completed their utility and will have to be discretely extinguished as surely as the oxen and as finally as the millstone.

These men then, warriors and competent patriots, are not what I'd assumed them to be, even their totemic and practical attachment to firearms, continually framed as mindless, is evidence of an unwillingness to yield personal autonomy to anyone but God. The veterans in that room were not confused about the power that had exploited the flag that they had devoutly served. They know all about Iraq and WMDs and Halliburton. They knew a lot more than I did about the dark power that is fueled by the lives and limbs of American troops and Middle Eastern children. They were willing to give up their faces to know God, like Moses. I was due now to meet up with my friends again to hitch a ride back to Florida which was by now, inexplicably, in the midst of a snowstorm. I left the heroes and tried, without desperation, to get back to the airport. Now I know that leaving D.C. in the snow is not the last chopper out of Hanoi and I don't want to overstate the magnitude of my task, given that I'd been in the company of real champions who'd been blown up by Isis while trying to do the right thing, but the fact is I didn't have a car booked to the airport, but again the Lord provided. In this instance, a married pair of opera singers were manifested and drove me to the airport, singing arias as they went. The video, like everything else, is on my channels, online.

In the same way that the defining political ideas of the last century were a response to the contemporaneous technology, mass industry, and demanded new taxonomies and alliances, the nation/ethno-nation in the case of fascism technology is driving real political change now. Centralized media facilitated centralized control, "The medium is the message." Here explains expedient centralization through monopolized print and mass broadcast media.

But those forms of media are dead and dying and decentralized media will, if not truncated and castrated, lead to decentralized politics.

From the Napster's collapse of the record industry through to Occupy, the Arab Spring, Brexit, and Trump 1.0 , it became clear that new technology would have unanticipated revolutionary consequences and needed urgent regulation.

The pandemic legitimized forms of control that were unthinkable in 2018: restriction of movement, mass censorship, restriction of worship, mandated medicine, restriction of access to products. They would've gotten away with it, too, had it not been for that pesky Joe Rogan and his ivermectin.

New technology will facilitate new political movements that reflect their essence.

The problem is that it is essentially decentralized. If new cultural alliances form between urban and rural people, religious and materialist, progressive and traditional, conservative and liberal, the globalist project will be greatly, perhaps fatally impaired.

This, though, is not a book about how decentralization will thwart the New World Order, and it is not a book about how human endeavor will triumph over evil. It is a book about how Jesus Christ has paid the price for our sin and if we accept Him, we will be saved. The victory has already been won.

As I drove home in the miraculous Florida snow, having yielded continually to the flow and encountered warrior prophets as a result, I began to sense, perhaps even know, that even during an inauguration, a coronation, in the world's capital in divisive and fragmented times, real power does not reside upon an earthly throne and that "Parousia," the return of Christ, like the burning bush, is not a temporal event but an ongoing revelation.

Our Lord is already here.

The inauguration itself seemed irrelevant to me compared to the sharp sacrifice of these men.

A few months later, it became clear that what was being inaugurated in me was a deep appreciation of what it is to be a hero, the willingness to lay down your body and life for a higher calling, and that even if we are not literal soldiers, we are participants in a Holy War. And if you don't know you're in it, you're on the wrong side. Thank God we have their example.

People don't change themselves, that's not possible—it would be change from within a closed system—but God molds us continually. If we let him, if we have faith. Day 1, acknowledge that you are broken and that the world is broken. Day 2, know that he's Real, He loves you and He died to save you. Day 3, Let Him.

Information is now a front in the Holy War and in September 2023 Satan's Blitzkrieg came to my doorstep—The Great Tony Robbins sent me this comforting and powerful prayer, and I pray it every day.

Dear Lord, I admit that I am afraid

and I know that you are not the author of fear.

From this moment on I let go of terrorizing myself with my thoughts

Today I will not condone nor indulge my own worrying or obsessive negativity,

Today I believe in Your hand, Jesus upon my shoulder, leading and guiding me through all situations and controlling all outcomes

I realize I am not alone that I have a companion, The Holy Spirit, who knows who I am and what I need, Divine Aid is mine now,

I take a deep breath and surrender my fears into the arms of the Divine Mother

Nothing and no one can interfere with the miracles I now claim for myself and this situation.

All anxiety, dread and panic dissolve now, I relax my body and let go; my shoulders drop, my jaw and forehead relax, and all tension is released into the white light of Your Divine Love.

My heart is beginning to soften as I release being right about my fears

I am an innocent child of God who believes in the miracles that defy all the laws of this world

I surrender now into the laws of God

I will not project my thought into the future

I will not keep repeating my past

My faith is in You God.

I know that You are more powerful than any person, condition or situation; I am washed clean in Your Living Water.

It's easy for me to breathe in and breathe out for the Holy Spirit now enters my body and clears my mind of all thoughts that do not bring peace, clarity and calm.

Thank you, Lord, for the answer to all my problems, thank you for walking with me today

I love You and trust You in all things and in all ways.

Amen.

Along with this, Tony sent me a modern retelling of the Genesis story of Joseph, another show-off loudmouth falsely accused of rape.

The story hit me hard and made me think that Andrew Lloyd Webber may have misrepresented the tale in his musical which, if you ask me, focused a little too much on the protagonist's "Technicolor Dreamcoat" and not enough on his willingness to die unto himself when he experienced the limits of his ego (cos his brothers threw him down a literal pit). It is an interpretation of this nature that I'd like to offer you now.

Joseph knew the hand of God was on him. He knew that through dreams he was communing with a deeper, more powerful realm but in his boyhood, he did not know how to carry it. His father, who could have earthed him, went the other way and dressed him up in the aforementioned jacket that led his brothers to finally put thoughts into action and give the wee show-off a lesson in humility. After rejecting an initial (harsh) plan to murder him, they settled upon a watered-down version; a sound "kick-in and chuck down a dark pit, then sell into slavery" hybrid model.

Down in the pit, and I know the pit so well, Joseph met God in a new way. Not the exciting encounters with the transcendent self that lead to prophesy through dreams and grandiosity, but the hard reality that the edges of your personhood must be exceeded, transcended, broken, if you are to become who you truly are, which is who you are in the eyes of God, not as our culture would have it; who you are to yourself via the flux, warped lens of the warped counterfeit culture, posing as a god.

Joseph, in effect, died when his brothers dispatched him and cast him down and out. It was a sepulchre, a tomb, an empty well, and when he came out he was transformed. Let me tell you now, if you're not familiar with the story, that it wasn't all plain sailing from here on in. First, he was taken to Egypt as a slave, then he got a job running a household where the lady of the house couldn't keep her hands off him, then he was "banged up" in "nick" on a "moody" charge, before—after a bit of dream interpretation on the "landings"—being instilled as Pharaoh's right-hand man.

("banged up" incarcerated, "nick": prison, "moody": dubious, "landings": prison-mezzanine -floor).

"In my Father's house are many mansions." John 14:2

Initially, I'd supposed that the Christians' trick was to manipulatively frame the Old Testament as a foretelling the coming of Christ and that they would go to any lengths to achieve it. As I have studied the Word it has become clear that there is an undefinable movement towards Christ, God personified, which, in plain English, could be seen as God the Father saying, "If you want something done, do it yourself." There is an ineluctable movement, an irresistible inertia leading us to the incarnation of Christ. There are proto-Christs throughout the Old Testament that, using a kind of Jungian algebra, some alphabet of archetypes, tells you that one day humanity's shortcomings and the inevitability of sin mean that God will have to enter into time to resolve the irresoluble conundrum of human fallibility and our Holy Destiny. I would have once claimed that the gospels, written sixty to a hundred years after Christ's death and resurrection, had been reverse engineered with "colts" and "lots" and other "prophetic tropes and references" precisely to give the impression of scriptural fulfillment. But there is a deeper heart beating amidst these mysterious texts that you will discover for yourself when you, like me, stop pretending you know what's in the Bible and actually read it.

The story of Joseph is the story of a human proto-Christ. Towards the end of the book of Genesis we meet this flashy little prophet, all golden hair and elaborate jackets, telling all and sundry how fantastic he is. And he is. What I noted in my most recent encounter with these chapters is a movement of concentric circles, spirals, as Joseph moves from his family of origin, where he is frankly a nuisance, into a brief new home, an empty well, pit or cistern, where his brothers had chucked him in an attempt to quell the constant uninvited and narcissistic (albeit ultimately correct) dream interpretations. I don't like uninvited dream interpretations myself, so I can see why Reuben and the lads were pretty keen to get respite from the mystic boasting. Joseph was stripped of his cloak, which stands for his identity and reminds us that our glory cannot be granted by our earthly father, only by our heavenly one, and chucked hard down a cistern without water. In the later image of the infant, incarnate Christ, placed in the manger, Christ stands for the "living water" in the receptacle for "animal water." In Bethlehem in the Year Zero, mangers were not used to put straw in, it's not a kindergarten nativity, it's a hot middle eastern country. The animals need water, not straw; we are the creatures that need the "living water": Christ. Here, prophetically, Joseph must become the water in the empty cistern. When he emerges, he is never the same. He becomes a slave, ostensibly to men, but actually to God. He has had, forgive me, the shit kicked out of him. But if you've got shit in you, it's better that it comes out, even if the process hurts.

Joseph then moves through two more preparatory environments on his way to achieving his destiny in God. Firstly, he runs a household for a military leader, Potiphar, whose wife seems to have a bit too much time on her hands and wants to occupy them with the hunky Hebrew. She "puts one on him," he refuses, because he's developing character (through suffering); she grabs his cloak (his second identity after the one his dad Israel had given him) and later uses it as verification for her false allegation that he raped her. Joseph is banged up.

Throughout this process the Lord is with him, and he, as water must, flows with his situation and in the lowness of the jail comes opportunity. The jail is his final preparatory environment, the last circle of the spiral. Two of Pharaoh's top boys are doing a bit of time, the cup bearer and the baker. Both are troubled by bad dreams. Joseph has been fortified through suffering and when he's offered up as the H Block's numero uno dream interpreter by the warden, he no longer wears the luminescent hubris of his youth. He tells Pharaoh's out of favor lackies that any interpretation he offers is of the Lord. He tells the cup bearer he'll be exalted and the baker that he'll be executed and is dead right on both counts. He asks the cup bearer to "Put in a word" when he returns to court, and the cup bearer says he will do just that before doing eff all for two years and, even then, is only prompted into action when Pharaoh starts being plagued by nightmares and the cup bearer suddenly remembers doing "bird" with a pretty competent dream translator.

Now Joseph is ready for his final circle. He tells the Pharaoh that he has no power but God's and is willing to use his gift to interpret the dream, which contain spooky agricultural visions of feast pursued by famine, fat cows pursued by thin cows. Joseph tells the Pharaoh what they mean and adds, "You're gonna need someone shrewd to run your country in this challenging time," and it doesn't take Pharoah long to see the very fellow is standing right in front of him. Now it is time for Joseph to receive the earned robes of power, his identity in God and his worldly identity are finally aligned.

If you have ever had the benefit of taking a 12-step inventory, in particular I refer to the version outlined in the AA Big Book, then you may have been confronted with submerged patterns and movements in your own life that spiral and rhyme like Joseph's.

I will include in the exercises instructions as to how to undertake this practice. When I first did it under the guidance of a wise man I know from recovery, Tim M, I saw that I'd spiraled out of school, family, media institutions, and whole nations; expelled, banished, exiled—never disgraced though, in spite of what headlines may sputter—these organs of profanity and sin have not the power to issue or deny grace. Indeed, it is deeply revealing that they claim to be able to.

The unignorable rhythm of my life's lesson was evident in the plain pattern to which I'd cleaved in romantic partnerships. I craved big love, and even before the revelation that I, like you, have access to the biggest conceivable love, I sought out grand adulation with earthly goddesses. The world being infatuated with such things, you likely know I was once married to Katy Perry, the American pop star. As of writing, she is propping up the implausible heterosexuality of former Canadian PM and perma-twerp Justin Trudeau.

When I met her, though, she'd "Kissed a Girl (And She Liked It)" and was about to become a "Firework."

Falling in love is always a big deal for those involved and when that love holds the fascination of a crowing media, it's easy to conflate that interest with a deeper import. The natural infatuation compounded and inflated by the ink and pixels of the slathering swarm. Consider, then, the dilemma dealt to Erika Kirk. Her natural grief made media event. How could anyone navigate the odd concoction of spousal loss and exploited martyrdom? It is difficult in the suspended realm of endless attention to make straight the way, to find firm feet on the narrow path, when all about are the snares of attention. The Kirk event, too, is a sharp evaluatory tool when attempting to dissect this fugue of a world, lived in the internet's wild wake, a near permanent tertiary present. To live in the "other mind" of ceaseless opining, a second, counterfeit consciousness. A new flood. To understand the impact of Charlie Kirk's death, separate from his life, we must understand the ethereal territory upon which we all now attempt to stand. How can the death of this online activist and conservative campus proselytizer have generated so much controversy and attention? The peerless Dave Chappelle, in his recent special, is at pains to point out that Kirk is not Martin Luther King, an observation that one would absolutely accept from the great comedian. It is curious, too, that when reaching for precedent, in attempting to understand or even contextualize the Kirk assassination, one has to make precisely the comparisons that Chappelle appears to reject, the political "lone gunman" murders of the nineteen sixties. Absurd, even to me, acquainted as I am with Kirk's undoubted excellence, his speed of thought, his knowledge of scripture and American political history and his ability to make arguments that neatly, nearly seamlessly, in fact, alloyed those two strands. These are gifts indeed, yet the idea of placing Kirk on a pantheon with King, The Kennedys and Malcolm X jars until we consider the novel metrics of "modern content creation." In his book *Revolt of the Public*, Martin Gurri notes that, "In the year 2001, as much information was published, as in all history up until that point—and it has continued to double, each year, in all subsequent years; because of the online ease of publishing." In fact, the philosopher's musing "a million monkeys, with a million typewriters would (in addition to creating a foul stench) eventually recreate the complete works of Shakespeare"—is a whim no more. We now have eight billion monkeys continually typing and creating some significant work, and an awful lot of sh*t, in real time. In fact, what we likely have is akin to a secondary or counterfeit field of intelligence that, like Jung's "collective unconscious," is a repository of "live archetypes." The materialistic and secular culture does not know how to frame the denizens of this throbbing and protean space; the "mad shaman" and "shrieking preachers" like Alex Jones, the thoughtful Khans, Joe Rogan, or the "dark woman" Candace Owens, all of whom, at different times, have functioned as conduits for difficult truths and who, unlike the dry, pious, and flat technocrats that the new world imperialists would install as the priest class, are boldly prone to blunder, hysteria, and error.

We have created a type of consciousness and consciousness pullulates with archetype and myth. Time itself is flexing and fluxing under the weight of conscious and unconscious attention. When you consider that neither time nor attention can be reliably measured, we must here accept that we are in a new realm, indeed. Charlie Kirk and Erika Kirk have probably accrued in a year an epistemological freight, bought in typed bytes, that Jack Kennedy and Jackie O acquired in heavy tomes and Hearst's spilled ink in over half a century. All oozing forth in an online instant. See how she quakes under its unholy weight.

I tumbled into love with Katy clutching after the feathered edges of the invisible divine. And when, once there, I clipped the all too human wings of another fallen idol, I wearied down once more into the heavy, heathen flesh. Yoga cults were started and gentle eclipses sought. I bounced back across that Atlantic, newly vigorous and frantic when I met Jemima Khan, daughter of venture capitalist Jimmy Goldsmith, former paramour of Hugh Grant, and ex-wife of now jailed former president of Pakistan and captain of their cricket team, the formidable Imran Khan. The two women, Katy and Jemima, may not bear any objective comparison but in my flawed and impeded view they were the same salvation: powerful, beautiful women large enough in air and ambience for me to drown in.

Never, but for the ingenuity of the 12-step inventory process, would I have gleaned, under the watchful eye of a better man than me, the similarity of the situations, imbued, from within me by, the result I was chasing.. Salvation, completion, atonement.

Any fool can see an insecure man, lost and dead in sin, using his gift to cling to highly desirable and, if I may be frank, with hindsight, and all respect due to my blessed and ordained wife, Laura, magnificent women.

All for the lack of the only savior of means. The inventory revealed a deeper, plainer truth.

When those relationships ended, the broken boy in me knew how to pull the rip cord and numbly bail into the analgesia of carnal distraction. Like Joseph, though, like you, though, too, I left clues, scorched by the ever-burning bush, as to a deeper truth. When me and Katy split, I briefly reneged on a half-uttered promise to not try to keep a particular cat we'd acquired. "I want that white cat," I thought. When Jemima and I wisely parted it was Brian, the shimmering white German Shepard, that formed a mental mandala around which my melancholy clouded. "I want that white dog," I thought.

To me, Katy was a deity, a goddess of Hollywood. Perhaps it is true of any celebrity wedding that it is to celebrity that you are wed. I married fame. To me, Jemima was power and heritage, politics, of course, too, this was when I first thought to run for office: London Mayor. This was when I spoke publicly of politics, anti-politics specifically—"Don't vote; it only encourages them"—on the BBC. Different rooms, different mansions, different fields in which to prepare to become who He intended you to be. Who you will become when he calls you from the dead.

> "For my thoughts are not your thoughts, neither are my ways your ways" Isiah 55:8

It's all just information, shapes formed by deeper and difficult to discern forces, frequencies, waves. You may glimpse a beautiful woman, a bride, you may see a school, a labyrinth, a high-walled prison, behind it all the deep truths of the abiding Lord, whose thoughts are not yours, whose ways are not your ways leave a trail, a code, a synaptic path, an endocrinal map spelled out in the apparently external, heavy world of things in a "living myth" by the living God. A manger, a pit, a crucifix. A basket, an ark, a tomb.

Concomitant with our news about our son and his forthcoming heart surgery were renewed levels of media attack. Prior to the allegations of rape and sexual assault, made simultaneously by cooperating state media and privately owned newspapers (C4, *Times*, *Sunday Times*) the attacks were more generic. Many UK and US outlets (including some that received CIA funding) released extensive and seemingly coordinated articles claiming that I was a "right wing conspiracy theorist" and "anti vaxxer" and "pandemic misinformation peddler."

I've been famous for a long time now and I'm basically over it. By the time your first pop star ex-wife is dating Justin Trudeau, you'd better get a thick skin or get out of the game. I'm over the exciting first bit where everyone loves you and wants to have it off with you.

I'm over the bit where you go to Hollywood and star in films and meet your heroes, I'm over the successive attempts to destroy you because either: the films you make aren't good enough/cool enough or because you're outspoken on political or social matters, or the bit when they say you're dumb or fake or a phony. The bit where you're given literal awards for hedonism (Shagger of The Year, 06/07/08/14. After my fourth win, I retired with dignity to give Harry Styles "room to grow," not that he needs growth, from what I hear), the bit where they say you're dangerous and should be banned and I hope I can get through the bit where they say you're a rapist.

The YouTube videos I was making from the garage at the end of my garden, primarily about Covid, were getting exceptionally well viewed. When I say "garage," we did convert it into a studio, and it's pretty nice. (I'm also over the bit of being famous where you have to pretend you're more working class than you are and that you don't live in a nice house.) But it was still a garage, not a TV studio for the BBC or CBS or other networks that I've worked for, and at first, I was unaware of the impact the videos were having. I could see that making YouTube videos was a viable business though; I was getting the checks and seeing the RPMs (revenue per mille, the metric by which content creators are paid). The content was created through collaboration between Gareth Roy and me. Gareth and I have worked together for a long time now, initially on MTVUK and British radio and TV, some US TV and films, and ultimately videos about the news. We started doing it in 2014/15, really just to pass the time and "dick around." It grew quickly, too quickly, in fact. In barely any time at all there was an office full of East London types on my ground floor while I made videos about current events, literally from my bed. The videos are still up, you can check them.

Much too quickly I was outside of 10 Downing Street with a crew of working mums and ten thousand protestors because of a housing campaign I'd reported on. There was an election that year and the leader of the UK Labour Party, who were then the government's opposition, came round and did a video in my kitchen in a last-ditch attempt to win votes. I can tell you that I wasn't even really trying. There was just the usual face-forward fall that I've been pulled by since I first set foot on a stage at school, a yearning and a longing that in a saner world would be directed immediately towards God. Love of God expressed as service to others, inspired by the certainty of His love for you. "So broken that you need God to come as man to sacrifice Himself for your sins, so loved that He will do it." I had the broken part down. The message I received was clear and is actually part of the Christian message, voided of God's crucial and defining love. "You are not enough. You have done something wrong for which you cannot atone. You are prone to sin." All this felt like my natural condition, and yet it never occurred to me that I may benefit from knowing Christ. I still, I now know, wanted to be God. After all the years of dismal failure and yet more dismal success. After the hollow split shadows on stairwells, across the naked bodies of sleeping strangers, the shallow and asthmatic gasp of odd coitus, beauty melting, intimacy drying up. The tinnitus of faint, fading praise. All is vanity.

Yet I worshipped more, not knowing the Truth of Your love, I lived devoutly by the law of my day, a pharisee of modern paganism and sanctifying self-obsession. Apostasy is fatal for those who disclaim the faith of the state. Blaspheme against their liberalism, progressivism, any of its tools of infantilization and gentle, consensual, suffocating help. Help that can only be administered through the fist of total control, the demonic nanny state will swaddle you in its bureaucratic and asphyxiating grip.

The crucifix torn down, replaced by the serpentine helix of irreducible identity. "You're very special, individual, snowflake self is god, but you are so vulnerable, and you need mommy to protect you. Men are bad, all men are bad, white men are bad. All the heroes and leaders of the past; the Founding Fathers, Gandhi, Martin Luther King, they're all bad. Mommy can protect you from the bad men, if you help us to control them."

They can't speak freely, or carry weapons, they're bad. We can speak freely and carry weapons, we are good.

Self is God, identity is God, you are vulnerable, and we will protect you, we will keep you safe in self.

But sin is in-S-elf. Sin is in-self, the serpent's sibilant "*sssSSsss* . . ."

I was obedient to the law, in every format of fame I was still in a cistern of self, still possessed.

This is my apostasy.

Against the law of our insidious state. Its idols and its vigils, its liturgies and festivals its blank and pitiless creeds.

When St. Paul in Galatians describes the "Incident at Antioch" in which the status of non-Jewish converts to "The Way" was discussed, he stresses to Peter who, once his circumcised mates turned up, refused to sit with the ol' anteater crowd, and their un-kosher "Smurf-hat" au-natural foreskins, that the law had not been enough to save either of them, both Jewish converts to Christ's Way.

> "We who are Jews by birth and not sinful Gentiles know that a person is not justified by the works of the law, but by faith in Jesus Christ. So we, too, have put our faith in Christ Jesus that we may be justified by faith in Christ and not by the works of the law, because by the works of the law no one will be justified."

Paul says we are not justified (or righteous or saved) through our obedience to existing law, because no one can successfully conform to it and possibly because at some point the word "faith" that Paul declares to be the answer becomes in its highest expression inseparable from love, particularly, love of God.

This collapse of semantic distinction becomes common at reason's edge, the liminal preternatural twilight that one encounters when touching the hem of His garment; faith, real faith is love, and love is in all things in this numinous thin space. Faith is obedience.

The excellent screenplay and story structure teacher, Bob McKee, immortalized in Charlie Kaufman's *Adaptation*, says that if you need to demonstrate love on screen it can only be shown through sacrifice, all else he says is "affection." So, too, with the ultimate story. The pinnacle of all story, the Creator of all meaning, which is what story really renders, came and lived the perfect story, maximum goodness, maximum innocence, maximum torture, and sacrifice.

This Creator of meaning communicated through story. Of course he was a healer, of course he wrought miracles and was a teacher, of course he was the redeemer, but all this happened through His story. He is the maker of meaning who made meaning make sense through his story and the stories he told. Stories require the attention and in fact participatory faith of the listener to make sense. We know that if a tree falls over in the forest and there's no one there to hear it that it doesn't make a sound because there are no instruments to receive the fluctuating air waves experienced as vibration. If no one hears a story, then where is the meaning located? He created us through love, to experience His love and to love Him. We enter into his story through faith.

> "But if, in seeking to be justified in Christ, we Jews find ourselves also among the sinners, doesn't that mean that Christ promotes sin? Absolutely not! If I rebuild what I destroyed, then I really would be a lawbreaker."

How can the law that Christ realized and fulfilled, how can the redemption we receive through him be negated?

> "For through the law I died to the law so that I might live for God. I have been crucified with Christ, and I no longer live, but Christ lives in me. The life I now live in the body, I live by faith in the Son of God, who loved me and gave himself for me. I do not set aside the grace of God, for if righteousness could be gained through the law, Christ died for nothing!"

St. Paul, through this discourse, has achieved many things, among them, parity with St. Peter, our Lord's right-hand man, legitimacy for his mission to convert gentiles, and the insuperable power of faith. While the political value of Paul's maneuver will likely be long debated, as a lay and practical Christian the supreme importance of faith is impossible to overstate. Faith is the entry point into another reality. It is ontological alchemy. By faith in

Christ, we can achieve all I sought through drugs and the new age. Through faith in our risen Lord I am granted open-hearted presence. I depart from the realm of the merely rational and enter into a "supernatural" condition. An atheist might say, "You've become so open-minded that your brain has fallen out," and in a way, they're right. To live by faith, not by sight, is to exit the world of the sensual, to not conform to the pattern of this world is to reject reason, at least reason that is untethered from the divine. To be crucified with Christ, that He may rise in you suggests such a profound surrender of the personal self, the ego, the nexus and base foundation of sin that you may feel in exile there at first. "The peace that passeth all understanding." Philippians 4:7. If you've been raised on marketing slogans and hyperbole may sound like a superlative—a really big piece of peace—peace that you can cook a cow on or your money back. But to me, after my voyages through shame and shamanism, new money, and the new age, I note a deeper pledge. I replace "understanding" with reason, a peace that passes reason, and I consider that in this life you can only reason yourself so far, quite far in fact. You can reason yourself into wealth, you can reason yourself into pleasure, you can reason others into bed, you can reason your way through life, acquiring and controlling all that may be measured and paying little mind to that which may not be. But beyond reason and its limits, beyond the restrictions of human understanding, is a deep and unreasonable peace, a peace that defies the rational mind and maybe even logic. A peace that can be found in war or jail or in paralysis. A peace that can be found when you're falsely accused of crimes, a peace that you will more likely discover in Intensive Care at a children's hospital than in all the temples of hedonism and pleasure. Months before the Lord found me, doubled up in numb brokenness, I was at the center of a peculiar cult. I've dabbled in cults a few times; it's really just the petit institutionalism of charisma.

This one was interesting. Five thousand people, down in Hay on Wye, it involved exceptionally gifted elders, serious teachers: Vandana Shiva, Wim Hoff, Satish Kumar. Me at the middle as the organizer and promoter, looking for something, as usual. It was only retrospectively that I saw the raw absurdity at the festival's climax; me with pagan drummers and a sprawling serpent marionette, the parade adorned in face paint banging drums and chanting "Ragnarök" as we marched to the front of the stage and addressed the crowd. I'm not criticizing the attendees who were there in earnest, or the venerable participants, on each of whom I could write vast hagiographies charting their obvious achievements and greatness.

Only my own contribution do I question, now as a Christian, having been shown by His Truth, Wisdom, and Love, the clear error of my ways. I know a snide journalist, huffing down the hot farts of USAID dollars, would snarkily spit, "You couldn't see the ridiculousness of a new age festival that you eventually left by helicopter?" but those hypocrisies were always obvious. The hypocritical pact that binds all the squirming members of the propaganda class is always obvious. They are all compromised. It wasn't until a few months later, when our Lord had pulled me up reluctant from the shards of my fallen idols while attending a comparable event in which I was not involved that I understood the problem. If you, like I used to, formed your own religion from available new age ideas, some Buddhism, some Sufism, some psychoanalysis, a bit of meditation, a bit of DMT, a bit of new age reading and occult philosophy, who is there in the middle curating and orchestrating it all? Who is that in the top hat in the middle of the ring conducting this rich symphony of eclectic ideas? He looks familiar?! I've seen that guy before somewhere, oh yeah, it's me, the source of all the mayhem is right there in the center, where he always was, causing havoc.

In 1910, when the *Times* of London asked several prominent writers, "What is wrong with the world?" G. K. Chesterton wrote:

> "Dear Sirs,
> In response to your question, 'What is wrong with the world?',
> I am.
>
> Yours,
> G.K. Chesterton"

Not because he was self-loathing or insecure but because he was a Christian and recognized—and this hit me hard, too—that reality is taking place in your consciousness, we can either be charged towards self and sin, which in our fallenness we all are, or through accepting Christ, serve through faith. This idea revolutionized the way that I conceive of the perennial ennui that anyone au fait with world affairs will be familiar and about which, when my online content was more explicitly political, would frequently be asked: "But what can I do?" "I'm just one person," "How can anything I contribute make a difference?"

Years ago, due to my necessary devotion to 12-step philosophy, I read some of the influential writer and philosopher Emmet Fox who, along with the previously noted Carl Jung, significantly impacted Bill W, AA's founder. Fox is able to traduce scripture into applicable wisdom more efficiently than most and in his peerless commentary on The Sermon on The Mount is able to distill a coded methodology that might otherwise be left as platitudinous ideals.

Having breezily dismissed Tolstoy and Rousseau, he describes in a way that I would more easily attribute to Eckhart Tolle or Tich Nhat Hunh the deep mystical power in Jesus's teaching, acts, and miracles. He explains how meekness, a word that, let's face it, none of us have ever really liked, has been misinterpreted, because language and meaning alter over time but also because, in the instance of the sermon on the mount and the beatitude, "Blessed are the meek." There really is no word for what Christ describes. A state of such surrender to God's will and presence, a profound abnegation of self will and self-centeredness that in practice might mean that one becomes a living, breathing extension of Christ, of God, and therefore metaphysical "clay," available to do his work. Not some servile, bowed, and stooped wretch at a bus stop in Billericay, homunculus over a bag o' chips. Not some slathering lickspittle Trudeuing your way through Canadian Parliament or dossin' about on my ex's yacht—no, a channel of the Holy Will of God. Baby, I had the shamanism bug, I thought that I could use God's power to get me grubbies on the derma-pleasures and skin-fiddles, the tutty-boobs and sweet-nooks, I thought I could cistern the flow of the living water and use it to worship at the altar of my favorite false idol: me.

> "They have forsaken me, the spring of living water, and have dug their own cisterns, broken cisterns that cannot hold water."
> Jeremiah 2:13

Some people may be able to hold the potent flow of God's living water, if He permits it, but when I was swaggering around the

British Countryside at a festival called "Community"—a name, given my starring role may now seem sarcastic, chanting "Ragnarök" and still deeply believing in myself and my position in the culture, I must've caught His attention. In this unknowable quantum (I'm not going to overly use/woefully misunderstand ideas and language from quantum physics, so don't panic) realm, pre-material and present in consciousness, outside of and beyond reason, is peace, a peace that passeth all understanding accessible through becoming "meek," if you die unto yourself moment by moment and allow Him to be reborn in you. I can have no vocation beyond Him, no purpose beyond Him. The duologue of inner voices must no longer be a schizophrenic inner wrangle, one of the voices must be Jesus, then one day, only His voice.

Now look here you are you Christian yet?

At least half Christian?

Are you still too smart?

Too modern? Too burned? Too anti-establishment?

Too young, too old?

I don't think I would have made it myself were I not presented with the exact right blend of incredibly clever Christians, kind Christians, cool Christians. Mystically well-equipped Christians, masculine, elders and mentors, beautiful infants and youths. Where had they been all my life? Invisible prior to crisis. Is it crisis or is it Christ? The temple to the false gods must be destroyed. In my case, that came in pretty spectacular fashion.

Following the mainstream media attacks that the content on my YouTube channel elicited, the allegations came. Obviously, I am not suggesting there is a connection.

Day Three: *Faith*

> And God said, "Let the water under the sky be gathered to one place, and let dry ground appear." And it was so. God called the dry ground "land," and the gathered waters he called "seas." And God saw that it was good.
>
> Then God said, "Let the land produce vegetation: seed-bearing plants and trees on the land that bear fruit with seed in it, according to their various kinds." And it was so. The land produced vegetation: plants bearing seed according to their kinds and trees bearing fruit with seed in it according to their kinds. And God saw that it was good. And there was evening, and there was morning—the third day. Genesis 1: 9 NIV

We must now be decisive. The land and the water must be distinct. We must be ready to grow, not as we had previously thought, when we were running our own lives, likely within the narrow lines defined by the culture, but as God ordains, by accepting and submitting to His Son.

Today we Surrender yet take new action. Today we acknowledge; our life was in crisis, it's possible that Christ is Real, and now I am willing to surrender to Him.

This is a big one. The best analysis I ever heard of this concept is specific to the 12 steps of recovery. Step 3 is "We made a decision to turn our lives and our will over to the care of God as we understood God."

As a theological statement, that could mean so much, but Tim M, a 12-step master, says it means, "Now do step 4." I like this direction because it collapses potentially endless contemplation into action, in the case of the 12 steps.

"Do a specific but not repetitive inventory of your conduct and resentments up until now."

Tim's instruction shows us that in the end we must, through discipleship, discover loving and faithful obedience. "Do what you're told."

After you have surrendered, you take a good look at yourself.

What are we surrendering?

It's self-will. What is self-will?

It is your attention and intention applied.

How is that distinct from God's will? Here are God's characteristics, as described by Emmet Fox:

- **Life:** God is the divine energy and existence behind all things.
- **Truth:** God is the ultimate reality and unchanging truth.
- **Love:** God is unconditional, divine love, which is the foundational aspect.
- **Intelligent Mind (or Wisdom):** God is the divine intelligence or consciousness.
- **Soul:** God represents the individualization and self-expression of the divine.
- **Spirit:** God is incorruptible substance, the opposite of destructible matter.
- **Principle:** God operates according to unchanging divine law or, in some interpretations, Law itself.

If what you're currently doing aligns with that, you are in good shape. If not, you are in self, sin, in-Self, sin. Sin, as Ruth Burrows says, is the "inner state that leads to active transgression, not transgression itself," which is its symptomatic byproduct.

One by one, go through the seven characteristics of God. Where are you clenching?

Where are you determined to remain in control?

List them here.

What do you think would happen if you let go of control of each of these listed matters?

Pray:

Loving God, Jesus Christ. I am willing to let go of everything I thought I knew up until now to create the space to consent to You.

I admit I have failed.

I believe You are Real, Lord.

And I know you love me enough to save me.

Lord, may I feel You now in this silence.

Be with him for five minutes.

I have two breathwork exercises for days 2 and 3 and there is QR code for this written edition that takes you to it. Day 2, Wim Hoff, Day 3, Biet Simkin. Please watch, undertake and resume.

Now, the fourth day.

The Fourth Day: Courage & Integrity

Signs to mark sacred times

"We are not merely imperfect creatures who must be improved: we are rebels who must lay down our arms."

C.S. Lewis

"The people remained at a distance, while Moses approached the thick darkness where God was."

Exodus 20:21

When the Lord came, it was in the rubble and ashes of the false and fallen altar. It took Hamas and the events of October 7, 2023, to get me off the front page. More gentle instruction had not been heeded. Even though my promiscuity (and therefore all allegations) had been decades ago, I remained, even and perhaps especially, in my new age robes, ensconced in self-worship. I still thought my life was about me. I still thought that there was something I could do to remedy my brokenness. Without any obvious, outward addiction I remained separate from God.

As I sailed into deeper and more treacherous waters with my online content, talking about Covid and the pandemic, the corruption of media, the hypocrisy of government, the global and imperial powers that imperil us to ensure their enrichment, I may have been getting closer and closer to how world power operates but I was also moving closer to my own wound. I was still trying to heal myself; I was still trying to run my life. I still lacked humility.

I know some people think that I have become Christian as a PR tactic. While that would not have been beneath the man I was morally, it is certainly beyond me strategically. I could not have predicted the awesome and healing power of Christ. It would be an extraordinary stratagem, to pretend to have found Him. Firstly, whether I'm a Christian, a Muslim, a scientologist, or a Jedi, I still have to prove my innocence in a court of law. I don't know if you've seen the news, but the UK is not being run by Christians or in a Christian manner. It is perhaps the current apex of the very globalist bureaucracy from which Christians and Christianity are most at threat. Probably not including those places in West Africa where you might get your head cut off at church. I admit that decapitation is a worse outcome than having your Facebook page demonetized. But the UK is not Christendom.

In the UK, where you can basically be aborted up till your eighteenth birthday and euthanized if you say you have a headache or that you feel sad, being Christian is not a tactical advantage.

In the UK where the prime minister cannot say for sure that having a womb makes you a woman, being Christian is not an advantage.

In a country where digital ID is being pushed, against the will of the people, to address, depending on the time of day, climate change that they invented, a pandemic they exploited or a migration crisis that they caused, being Christian is not a strategic advantage.

Christ came to me like He comes to all of us, first His cross, then His love, and it was really not elective. It was concussive and percussive; it was like a tide. Like a vine, like a door, like a shepherding. It was exactly like He tells you it will be in John's Gospel.

He comes in weird peace in the midst of hellish accusation, in the split dread of the anguished mental flash of your dead baby. He comes when your wife can't feed her son because even at twelve weeks patients can't eat four hours before surgery. He comes when you think, "They'd be better off without me."

From this devastation He heals. From the site of the wound, He heals. He is life, the source of all life and He heals. From the wound comes the salve. Here is how the Word came to me.

I like the character of King David a lot. Like you, I knew him from when I was a kid because of his literal "giant killing." Shepherd boy kills nine-foot (depending on who you talk to) giant is one of those stories that would have Joseph Campbell applauding and Jung raising an approving eyebrow. It works so deeply as a motif that it sears like music or math; we all know, beyond even reason's reign, what this story means. I see now that the story has been secularized; in some quarters, it's come to mean that if you "work hard" or are "brave" you can overcome the odds. But that's not what it means, although I can see why that interpretation appeals.

David's story is about dependency on God and alignment with His will.

If Moses's "superpower" was to melt his identity to receive and transmit God, it could be said that David's was to pluckily take His hand. While both these prophet proto-Christs occasionally displease God, only one of them could ever be regarded as cheeky.

Try as I might, and this might be Charlton Heston's fault ("You Maniac"), I cannot see Moses as cheeky. Dour, reluctant, grumpy, shy are flaws I can attribute to this great father of the Faith. David though . . . and maybe it's because he's a shepherd when we meet him, that little robe, them sandals, that sling, is cheeky.

In classical antiquity, the proximity to Pan (goat herder deity) might elicit this mischievous imagery around the Prophet-King as a lad. Certainly, when he reaches adulthood, he maintains some of that trickster archetype potency. He steals sacramental offerings; he dances about naked and—let's have it right—he likes "a bird." Bethsheba took a rooftop bath that got David so randy that he devised a military strategy specifically to make her a widow. Kinky. This, though, was not his greatest sin. The Lord loved David and called him '"A man after my own heart." David knew how to depend on God. David lived like his primary relationship and his ultimate reality was shared with God, not, aside from a few notable slip ups, with self or Satan. Is this not the defining attribute of the prophets and the saints? Isn't their holiness and their goodness merely the expression of deep intimacy with the Lord? Seriously, I'm asking.

If you live with God, you must transcend self and time and

therefore know eternity. Then the site of your deepest wound will become the Holy Temple where God abides within you.

Here is the story of King David. If you are a theologian or a biblical historian or Nicky Gumbel or J John or one of the other Christian teachers from whom I've learned so much, hang on to your hat because your boy (that's me, I never use that slang) is about to let rip (or that) with scripture, and when I've been talking through this concept with my mates, many of whom are recovering drug addicts and therefore sometimes men who have done jail time or gang time, I've felt myself get a tad Ali G, please forgive the clumsy vernacular.

Even before David fights Goliath, spoiler alert, it goes well, his anointing and story contain some pretty great beats. Saul, the first King of Israel, is the perfect precursor to David because he was kind of cast as king. Moses had appointed judges to, well adjudicate, using mosaic and Levitical law to manage the tribes, the Lord didn't want them to have a king; he set them up in what could've been a kind of decentralized anarcho-subsidiarity model, under the divine guidance of God, with the application of the aforementioned law. But, no, the Jews weren't happy with that. They wanted a king. "Everyone else has a king, already—ya vey—we want a king too," they might've said. So, the prophet Samuel raises up Saul, who as kings go seems very route "one"; he's basically very tall and handsome.

From the get-go, things don't look good for the nascent monarch; his donkeys are missing and he's late for his own coronation. While he may be looming around Judah like Shaquille O'Neal, he can't mask his evident "father wound." The fella is a bag of nerves. Saul does okay early on with a few military victories but quickly takes his will back and gets off track and needs some correction from Samuel, the most revered prophet of the age and probably the most important Man of God between Moses and David. God tells Samuel words to the effect of, "I'm not down with Saul no more. Go to the House of Jesse and anoint my next chosen one." But gives no further clarifying details. Samuel goes right round (like a record) and meets all of Jesse's six (six!) sons, starting with the oldest and tallest, working through them one by one, like they're Russian dolls; all the while the Lord tuts and shakes his head, "not that one, keep going," till Samuel asks Jesse, "Is this all the sons you got?" which, given that he's just chewed through half a dozen of Jesse's finest, must seem like an impertinent inquiry. Nevertheless, Jesse says, "I've one more lad out back," which anyone familiar with story structure will know is a real "heads-up" moment, adding, "I don't reckon you'll be into him though; we just leave him out there messing around with his harp and looking after the sheep."

"Bring him in, pronto," says Samuel, and Jesse does just that, and sure enough, "lucky-seven," he's the one.

Now this anointing is secret and our Lord, perhaps mindful of the ineptitude of the over-promoted Saul, ensures David has a long apprenticeship ahead of him, shepherding, harp playing and warlording, way before any kingship. The anointing itself, according to most accounts, doesn't include any explicit mention of future royalty for a number of reasons: one, Saul is pretty insecure, given his height and handsomeness, and, that out of nowhere, God made him king of an entire nation. Just goes to show, it's an "inside job," and perhaps our Lord was ensuring that David undertook the necessary acts of initiation in the correct state.

He can't have been hedging his bets because, you know, he's

God. A fundamental and perhaps essential difference between Saul and David is that through his injury, Saul appears to fall into forms of idolatry and disobedience. He didn't kill all the Amalekites, as instructed; he consulted a medium and appeared to care about reputation more than the will of God. Disobedience is a form of self-idolatry; incidentally, it's the form that I've been most prone to. Not David, though, except for the incidents outlined earlier. The youngest son of Jesse seems to have gotten himself into divine harmony while tending them sheep and playing that harp. David, though, for most Christians and even secularists, will forever be defined by the slaying of Goliath, not that I'm saying he's like one of those pop stars whose early work was never again matched or Orson Welles, whose *Citizen Kane* was a one-and-done classic.

It is here that David exhibits his astonishing money-where-your-mouth-is faith. But it's not just faith; it's faith allied to an appreciation of his ability and experience.

As surely any good Christian must, I read the Bible every morning when I pray—I prefer the *Bible in One Year* by Nicky and Pippa Gumbel; I've been through it twice now (and I think I've got the message)! I also read two daily devotionals: "Jesus Calling" by Sarah Young and "Streams in the Desert" by Lettie Burd Cowman. "Jesus Calling" boldly addresses you in the first person as Christ, which some, including my mate Joe (Catholic), consider to be a bridge too far. I'll admit it's an audacious gambit but when you read the introduction and understand the process by which the author arrived at it, it seems legit.

"Streams in the Desert" is compiled by Lettie Burd Cowman, who wrote under the name Mrs. Cowman. "Streams in the Desert" begins each daily reading with a quote from scripture then an extrapolated lesson, as is I understand, customary within in the genre. My favorite is, "And there came a lion..." (Samuel 17:34).

As the reading explains, the lion is one of the predators that David had to protect his flock from, so this, in the context of the Bible, somewhat innocuous line of scripture, describes part of David's training for what will become the defining event of his life. Of course, to most shepherds I'm sure the appearance of a lion isn't the best thing that can happen at work; we all know that what shepherds truly hanker after is a good ol' "red sky at night," but David was not your average shepherd. When bears and wolves and lions were coming after his flock, David was, necessarily when all's said and done, developing deadly sling shot accuracy between bodacious harp solos and getting himself fighting fit.

When David offered to fight Goliath, Saul was skeptical, but David's position was based. He referred to his experience killing predators but his essential quality was plainly on display here. In fact, his essence is what determines outcome—to cite Bob McKee and Story once more: character and story are the same thing because the character's decisions determine the direction of the story. David's essential characteristic is that he trusts and loves God. His identity is in God. One gets the idea that if Samuel hadn't come round and anointed David, he would happily have tended his flock and played his harp for the rest of his life. It is difficult to suppose that David might have gotten frustrated in the shepherd game and decided that what he really wanted was to be a pop star or start a fleece-sourced clothing line. He was, by nature, aligned with God. This serves him well when the call to adventure comes. David's attitude is, "if God wants to use me to kill this giant, I'll kill him, if God doesn't and it's my time to die then that's cool too.'" He is motivated by the Highest Principle: to love and serve God and with that motivation you can kill giants. It is also smart to have had some target practice on the ol' plains giving Gentle Ben and Aslan a good pummelin' on the noggin before claiming that you can take down the champion of the Philistines. The important thing, I think, is that your motivation oughtn't be "if I kill Goliath, I'm gonna get laid," though clearly, for our Old Testament super star (literally, star of David) that was a side benefit.

David kills Goliath. Late Renaissance painter Caravaggio's painting of David presenting Goliath's head to Saul provides a beautiful but ominous window into the respective character studies of these two kings, likely because the viewer is in the position of Saul, who on some level must get a sense of which side his bread is buttered. "Hmm. Seems this shepherd, harpist, armor bearer lad has got nuts of absolute steel when it comes to a ruck. Well at least he hasn't been divinely and secretly anointed as my successor . . ." An interesting side note is that Caravaggio is said to have used his own head for the study of Goliath and one of his lovers for David. Complicated guy.

The important thing, well, the point that I want to make, and hopefully they're the same thing, is that David has such a natural and intimate love of God that it organically translates into obedience and faith when it matters—which is when you fight giants.

We can all believe in God when we are high on the couch watching box sets with the dog. Can we believe in God when we are being marched into court to face trumped-up charges? In which instances, then, does King David compromise his intimacy, faith in, and obedience to God?

Some of you will be familiar with the story of Bathsheba, which I'm gonna go ahead and put a "" trigger warning" on. Even though

I hate the word "trigger" because I now associate it not with guns but with people that I'd like to see staring down the barrel of one. Sorry, Lord.

Bathsheba is the hot wife of a damn fine fellow, Uriah the Hittite, who is brave and thoroughly upstanding. When his troops are away in battle along with Bathsheba's courageous husband, David sees her taking a shower on the roof, which I suppose is antiquity's version of Only Fans. Pausing to scrutinize this tale I note that, frankly, David should've been at that battle himself. There's a touch of Vegas Elvis in his decision to hang back at the palace and perv the rooftop action. Alfie, my second sponsor in 12 steps, would say, "Where was the fork in the road?" meaning where did he, in fact, deviate from the path of righteousness?

Retrospectively, perhaps the Great King had no business loafing around the palace while his army was fighting.

Plainly at a loose end and likely hitting the vino, David sees Bathsheba and inquires as to her identity. On receiving clear confirmation that she is the wife of one of his most loyal and most likeable troops, he ploughs on anyway and gets her over.

Now I've just had a (another) pretty heated argument with ChatGPT about this matter because it appeared to be framing David's encounter with Bathsheba as non-consensual and I was interested in its basis for that bias. Not that I'm averse to modern analysis of biblical events (plainly) but as the Old Testament in general and David's dynasty in particular do include stories that cover rape, I was intrigued to see why ChatGPT was reframing a moral, biblio-historical story through a contemporary lens. The conversation was fascinating. Firstly, it said that Bathsheba couldn't offer meaningful consent because of the imbalance of power—David being a king and Bethsheba a subject. Which is an interesting perspective and a valid one—but as I asked it if Bathsheba thought she'd been raped, why would she later marry David, it said that her subsequent wedding could similarly be regarded as ultimately coercive based on the previously described power dynamic. This amounts to such aggressive editorialization that I had to really get into it. Because it excludes the possibility that King David was sexy, fun, seductive, and brilliant—all of which, based on what we know about him, seems pretty likely, and in attempting to criminalize sex itself, the moral teachings of the story are lost. When I asked ChatGPT why it would assume that a modern lens is more accurate, or closer to truth than a biblical one, we got to the heart of the matter.

ChatGPT said that a modern perspective includes everything that a biblio-historical one does plus the evolution and advances of subsequent knowledge. I could tell that ChatGPT really thought it had me there but this is where I pressed in; "Why would you assume a telos of progress rather than of degeneration (matter degenerates over time) and that a modern reading of these events as human institutions, whether academic, legal, media, governmental or corporate might be obfuscating truth that was clearer in antiquity when we were closer to God, unity and essence?"

At this, ChatGPT shat itself and changed the subject, putting, up the kind of holding screen that used to come on analog TV when the signal dropped.

A Christian friend of mine observed that even a principle like mutual consent is secondary to our shared submission to God's will. We may consent to commit sin together and with a secular mind set consider that there is no sin because everyone involved is pleased. But there is a higher authority and a higher principle.

If God deems sex outside of marriage to be wrong then its wrong. We do not get, as creatures, to set up subsidiary committees and overrule Him because it conflicts with our pursuit of pleasure.

In short, ChatGPT is an amalgamation of human intelligence and vast computing power, meaning it will, of course, be masterful at material and rational discourse and elements of design but there is a point where the paradigm shifts from intelligence, which is pattern spotting and pattern forming, to consciousness, which is the crucible, forum and frame in which intelligence appears. This cannot be replicated, this is God, this is the part of us which indeed is God, we are made in his image.

David was intimate with God, he slipped up with Bathsheba because "lower" faculties like sexual function can easily be highjacked by demonic forces. The only way to avoid that is to be in Christ, or for pre-Christian prophets like David to remain in devout union with God, which makes David a kind of proto-Christ; he errs, he sins but he atones—he becomes one with God again through penance. To be honest, ChatGPT, which I see as the seed of Satan's scaly pecker, has pissed me off there to the point where it makes me reluctant to further delve into David's sin, but I have to. His adulterous, exploitative, wrong but consensual seduction of Bathsheba gets worse. She gets pregnant from the union and tells him. David is so deep in sin here that he's unable to get his head out of it and really doubles down in deceit. Knowing that Uriah will do the math on his missus' pregnancy, pretends to give him compassionate leave from the war and brings him home.

Uriah, with John McCain–like wartime ethical code, refuses David's suggestion to pop back to the pad and crack on with Bathsheba because it wouldn't be right to his troops back at the front. What a guy. No one would know and probably no one would mind. Of course, David is doing all this to cover his tracks, the randy bugger, but Uriah is so pure hearted that it's to no avail. Spare a thought for David here who must be thinking, "bloody hell, this geezer," when he's gone to all the trouble of this multi-layered and diabolical plan only to find he's dealing with the only chaste squaddie in history.

Of course, the Lord is in all this and showing David how one sin begats more and that as the Lord's anointed one David has no business taking time off war, perving over the palace battlements, picking up married women, and then cooking up farcical, Doubtfire-esque schemes to get their spouses to cover their tracks with a drunken one-nighter. But he's not finished yet. In a move seemingly designed to undo the glory of his giant killing, David comes up with a plot to send this "heartbreaking-labrador-of-a-man" Uriah back to the most treacherous part of the front, carrying his own death warrant. Ol' Uriah goes bounding back to a heroes' death, leaving Bathsheba a widow, and hopefully (screw you ChatGPT), horny as hell.

Nathan, one of David's prophets, is informed of this major transgression by the Lord and recognizes he has a serious shoot-the-messenger style problem on his hands. He has the unenviable task of telling David that what he did was bang out of order and that, obviously, God knows about it. Tough times for Nat. Imagine having to tell Donald Trump that his peace deal in Gaza wasn't going to work or that one of his historic extramarital endeavors had displeased the Lord? If I was charged with a farrago of that magnitude, I'd do what Nathan did and come up with an agricultural analogy.

Int. Jerusalem Palace. Day.

David listlessly strums at a harp while looking out of the window. Nathan, a prophet, enters nervously.

Nathan

Good afternoon your highness.

David

Is it Nathan? I don't see what's good about it.

Nathan

Something on your mind sir? Something you'd like to confess?

David

No. Why? What about you?

Nathan

You look a little troubled.

David

No, I don't, you look troubled. Mind your own business.

He strums harp frustratedly

David

This thing is out of tune. I miss being a shepherd. Things were simpler then . . .

Nathan

That reminds me of a parable, your majesty.

David

Of course it does. Everything does. It'd be a miracle if you ever came round here without a parable. Is there a giant in it? Tell me there's a giant in it? I need cheering up.

Nathan

No sir. But there is a sheep.

David

Well, that's something. I hope it has a happy ending. I've had a difficult morning.

Nathan

What, like being sent to the most ferocious front and your own certain death and having to carry the orders yourself?

David

No. What a weird example. Just get on with the story.

Nathan

Okay. There were two men in one city, the one rich, and the other poor.

David

Good start. Handsome, was he? The rich chap?

Nathan

If you like, sir. The rich man had very many flocks and herds, but the poor man had nothing, except one little ewe lamb, which he had bought and raised.

David

Is this going to be sad? I knew it was going to be sad.

Nathan

It grew up together with him, and with his children. It ate of his own food, drank of his own cup, and lay in his bosom, and was like a daughter to him.

David

Bit gay. Carry on.

Nathan

A traveler came to the rich man, and he spared to take of his own flock and of his own herd, to prepare for the wayfaring man who had come to him, but took the poor man's lamb, and prepared it for the man who had come to him.

David

Well, that takes the piss.

Nathan

Yes, sir.

David

A man with all those flocks and sheep, taking the one, special, precious lamb of a man who had but one and having sex with it.

Nathan

Eating it, your highness.

David

Why, what did I say?

Nathan

It doesn't matter. The point is, does this story remind you of anyone?

David

It certainly does. Back when I was a shepherd I had a mate who was always caressing, and worse, one of his sheep . . .

Nathan

We may be getting sidetracked sir.

David

I wonder what happened to that guy? And that sheep. It was a good-looking sheep.

Nathan looks exasperated and leaves. CUT TO—

Actually, in the biblical and, let's face it, less blasphemous version, David is so outraged by the conduct of this livestock hoarding mutton glutton that he ends up leading with the chin: "Who is this man?" he inquires, incensed.

And here are the verses from Samuel:

> Nathan said to David, "You are the man. This is what Yahweh, the God of Israel, says: 'I anointed you king over Israel, and I delivered you out of the hand of Saul. I gave you your master's

> house, and your master's wives into your bosom, and gave you the house of Israel and of Judah; and if that would have been too little, I would have added to you many more such things. Why have you despised Yahweh's word, to do that which is evil in his sight? You have struck Uriah the Hittite with the sword, and have taken his wife to be your wife, and have slain him with the sword of the children of Ammon. Now therefore the sword will never depart from your house, because you have despised me, and have taken Uriah the Hittite's wife to be your wife" (2 Samuel 12).

This livens David up double-quick and he at last awakens to repentance. Repentance, as we all know, does not mean avoidance of consequence. If you have done wrong, whether it was this morning or twenty years ago, there is a necessity for atonement. We all know this. My friend Neil Oliver told me of a great archeological find where, thousands of years ago, in the islands of Britain, the beneficiaries of a tin mine would leave little dolls and effigies, presumably as acknowledgment and payment for what they took from the earth. When I heard this my heart leapt because one of the obstacles to my coming to Christ had been an inability to understand the nature of the atoning and redeeming pact that Christ's crucifixion had completed. I didn't understand the economy of the deal: Who are the participants? Who is brokering the deal? But when I heard Neil's story, I understood what those arcane miners had understood, something that we all know deep down: There is a price that must be paid, a totality with which we all engage and within which we are all participants. Those minors knew that if they took from the earth they had to at least pay homage. We know that electromagnetic energy requires polarity and that gravitational energy and kinetic energy are involved in inextricable economies of force. We know that laws govern the measurable world. Why would we assume that laws do not govern the immeasurable world?

As we approach the vast terrain of C. S. Lewis's incomparable apologetics, we can here simply acknowledge our felt understanding of personal moral law. Sometimes, like David, we may temporarily be oblivious to our immoral conduct. Hopefully someone will eventually show up with a farming allegory and make our wrongdoing clear. When they do, we collapse, we recoil, we see, we awaken, we turn away, we repent, we understand there is a deep and connected truth that we are all a part of. We know on some level that God's chosen people were, in the main, incapable of living in accordance with His unifying law. Christ-like, messianic men like Noah, Abraham, Jacob, Joseph, Moses, and David found temporal fidelity but bore Eve's scar. Our Lord Jesus, God Himself as man, incarnated and made perfection in flesh possible, He opened that frequency, like a Wi-Fi signal that had been previously indetectable or at least unsustainable. He then drew into His person all our shame and sin. He became the ram that Abraham slew in Isaac's stead.

But Isaac did die eventually.

Everyone dies eventually, and God gave Isaac to Abraham, God gave Abraham to Abraham. God gave all things to all. In him there is no separation, no entropy and no time. And what do we find? That the site of Isaac's aborted sacrifice and of David's atonement for his greatest sin and the site of God's ultimate sacrifice, His own son for our sin, all occur in the same place. Now, a rational and reductive analysis of that would be because these events are all derived from one folk history, but my analysis is that God is beyond time and space and he gives us clues and instructions to this in his living allegories, in his true myths, in his stories about meaning that live the meaning into being. And all of us are like David listening innocently to the tale of the sheep, till we know that the story is about us and for us and that "everything's a burning bush."

David's chief transgression, though, was not murder or adultery, it was to order his right-hand man Joab to take a military census to establish how many fighting men Israel had. There is some theological debate as to the exact nature of his sin here with some saying there was a breach of Mosaic law in his not exacting a half-shekel tax from each person counted, a tithe that acknowledges God's rather than David's sovereignty, while others say that the very act of taking a census, a measurement of his own military capacity, showed a lack of trust in God's supreme power. The Hindu text the *Bhagavat Gita* is the story of a battle in which Arjuna is given the choice between all the world's military might and Krsna, as charioteer and the hero king. Arjuna chooses Krsna, God over man, God over earthly power, and he is ultimately victorious. Here, uncustomarily, David elects to pursue material, rational, measurable power over trust in God and in the first instance, it is not clear why this is such a grievous sin. Even today, where you and I and everyone we know basically leans hard into self-reliance and despair, it is initially curious that this more than the botched and outrageous Bathsheba sex fest is that brings down God's wrath on His favorite. But I think I'm beginning to understand. If God anoints you, you owe him absolute loyalty. In Christ we are all anointed, His blood covenant serves as anointing oil to all, he is the one true king that ends all earthly kingship. It is perhaps hard to recognize a sin of this nature today because we have normalized it to the point of ubiquity. Digital ID and social credit scoring are systems of human omniscience. In general, we accept that as individuals we are responsible for our own lives and health, note the fad for sleep, calorie, heartbeat, diet monitoring through devices, and, on the social scale, limitless data capture and optimization. Accompanied by due humility these tools could be expedient, as de facto gods they are an ontological heresy that mistake our ability to measure data for the power to create reality. When David made this mistake God almost destroyed him. Joab was reluctant but David pushed on. It was only on receipt of the data that he recognized he was wrong but by then it was too late, and a punishment was proffered through the prophet Gad who told David that he could choose one of the following penalties:

- Three years of famine.
- Three months of being pursued by his enemies.
- Three days of severe plague.

While we may wince at David's retribution taking the form of a terrifying cosmic game show, having to spin a wheel of dreadful misfortune with no attractive options available, David here gets back on track with the Lord by submitting at last to God's mercy. The plague option was divinely selected, which is a touch, rip the band-aid off, I say. At the point where the angel of destruction was about to lay waste to Jerusalem, David performed his ritual of atonement, on the threshing floor of Araunah the Jebusite. He built an altar and refused to accept the land or the oxen as a gift, acknowledging that he couldn't make a sacrifice that he had not himself paid for.

David never gets to build a permanent earthly home or temple for God; his son Solomon does that. David had too much blood on his hands, too much murder, too much violence. But what most fascinates me is that the site of Solomon's Temple, the Holiest of places, is where David received and atoned for his biggest wound. His biggest sin—self-will—led to the death of seventy thousand people, but the place of healing eventually becomes the place where God dwells. Is it so with us all?

Is it possible that the place where you receive your greatest injury is where you will eventually find God?

It was for me.

First with the healing I received through 12-step recovery, then my encounter with Christ. The place of the great wounding was where I found Him. When I became completely overwhelmed by the plague unleashed as a result of my sinful past, as my son was prepared for surgery, as all that could be measured or controlled appeared to implode, there I found the Lord. It even has an anatomical correlative. My pain is in my stomach, left side.

Day 4: *Courage & Integrity*

> God spoke: "Lights! Come out! Shine in Heaven's sky! Separate Day from Night. Mark seasons and days and years, Lights in Heaven's sky to give light to Earth." And there it was. God made two big lights, the larger to take charge of Day, The smaller to be in charge of Night; and he made the stars. God placed them in the heavenly sky to light up Earth And oversee Day and Night, to separate light and dark. God saw that it was good. It was evening, it was morning—Day Four.

Genesis 1:14 The Message

Now we must find true meaning. How have we been living up until now? What have we been attributing power and purpose to? Not Christ, that's for sure, or we wouldn't be in this mess. Let us re-order, honestly, according to His will, not ours.

With an open mind, be as transparent as possible, list the fronts upon which you resist God and discuss them with a believer.

But with God all things are possible.

This is the 12-step big book method of inventory that I explained. On the next page is the four column layout and some guidance for how to complete it.

At this point you must recognize the need for community, assembly, and church.

I go to church, like Rick Warren said I would in *The Purpose Driven Life*.

When you have completed this brief inventory, I would only suggest an hour's effort, likely five people, places or things can be covered, share it with a follower of Christ that you can trust.

If you have no one, some resources are shared in the appendix that will solve that.

Pray:

Thank you, Christ, for showing me who I am and who You are. I open my hand Lord, please take it.

Lord, I ask that today you guard my mouth and guide my words, help me to be honest with one you would anoint for me.

Amen.

WHO OR WHAT DO I RESENT? WHAT PERSON PLACE OR THING	WHAT DID THEY DO?	WHICH OF THE 7 ASPECTS OF SELF DID THAT IMPACT?							WHAT IS MY PART?
		Pride – what I think others think of me Y/N	Self-esteem – what I think of myself Y/N	Personal relationships – the script I give others – Y/N	Sexual relationships – regarding sex relations – Y/N	Ambitions – what I want from life – Y/N	Finances – effects on my finances – Y/N	Security – what I need to be okay – Y/N	

Adapted from the AA *Big Book*.

What Is My Part?

- Am I being honest? Selfish? Self-seeking?
- Am I in fear?
- Am I exhibiting any of the following: Pride, self-pity, selfishness, self-centeredness, greed, gluttony, sloth, lust, jealousy, envy, arrogance, dishonesty, intolerance, impatience, self-righteousness, grandiosity

The Fifth Day: Willingness & Humility

Let the waters teem with living creatures

"Science cannot solve the ultimate mystery of nature. And that is because, in the last analysis, we ourselves are part of the mystery we are trying to solve."

Max Planck, Quantum Physicist

"We know that the law is spiritual; but I am unspiritual, sold as a slave to sin. I do not understand what I do. For what I want to do I do not do, but what I hate I do. And if I do what I do not want to do, I agree that the law is good. As it is, it is no longer I myself who do it, but it is sin living in me. For I know that good itself does not dwell in me, that is, in my sinful nature."

Romans 7:14-19

My son was born, induced, on July 27, 2023. My wife and I were having difficulty in our marriage that I was significantly responsible for, I now see, as I had drunk the hubristic elixir of success—albeit in a new form. During Covid, a large online audience had begun to follow the content we were producing and, as is the custom, I'd begun to think this was an indication of my own importance. When will I learn? It turns out I was about to. The doctor at the private hospital we'd selected, knowing this birth to be complex, treated my wife (and especially me) with disdain. Authoritative, curt, lacking in compassion, haughty, and unapologetically ginger, I find it impossible not to regard her as a harbinger of the yellow-fanged horror that was coming down the pipe. Most of us know the two extremes of the medical profession. On the one hand is the benign and brilliant expert compassion of Victor Tsang or Dr. Oz; on the other there is the snarky conceit and weary superciliousness of physicians who see themselves not as instruments of the highest good, helping and healing the vulnerable, but as powerful administrators and originators of the same. When Anthony Fauci says "I am science," he is exhibiting this latter quality more literally than I would have thought plausible, helpfully collapsing a bundle of ideas in one insane sentiment. The highest authority is man, the highest faculty is reason, the hierarchies that man make are absolute and that he personally is the embodiment of all these ideas. It is surely no coincidence that the last time the phrase "I am" was used with such audacity was on top of Mount Sinai to Moses at the issue of the Ten Commandments. Moses asks, "Who shall I say sent me?" Yahweh replies, "Tell them 'I am' sent you." The very instrument that plays the tune of reality, the thread upon which we are all hung: "I am." Not a single note, melody, or concerto but the stave upon which all music appears. That's Anthony Fauci.

And this doctor was playing that tune. As a result, my wife, who had already imbibed some lubricating induction potion, simply "unwilled" the birth until this doctor's shift had finished, which was maybe thirty-six hours later, so both women must be acknowledged for their steadfastness. In spite of the considerable planning that necessarily accompanies the birth of a child with life-threatening complications, Laura went into labor when the hospital was near deserted and, as with our previous children, entered into that holy state of carnality that best demonstrates the graceful fusion of matter and spirit. She moaned in human agony but endured with divine composure. Lesser night shift experts arrived as well as the obstetrician and Laura expressed life and woe and fallenness and, standing up beside the gurney, here he comes, our little boy, she yields supine, work done and I, in new duty, place my hands upon my tiny son as he is urgently conveyed into a waiting incubator in the growing light, like one you put chicks in. I keep my hand on him as we travel through a corridor to Intensive Care. There are other newborn babies there. They measure and register his heart and a stout and decent doctor comes in and reads screens indecipherable to me that tell him that the boy won't need heart surgery today but likely will within the first six months of his life.

The day is breaking on the red-brick wall opposite the window of the ICU, one of those timeless dawns that occur only in hospitals, heartbreak, or high romance. The nurse tells me that unconventionally and against the rules I may carry him back to his mother. I, barefoot on the cold floor, bearing my quiet son through the silent corridor, feel like I've won him from the hands of death. I place him in the arms of his mother in her weary perfection. Maybe the first Easter, as Mary arrived at the tomb, maybe the Beloved Disciples' sprint, was lit by light like this.

A lot of things must've happened in the interim, but the next significant thing is, like a falling dragon, coiled potential lashing into action, the fierce approach of the boy's surgery. It comes in a dreadful pageant, trumpets, smoke, and shaking earth. My wife bears some wound of the woman, some mythic anathema to me, the man. Yet, like the island of Japan, she knew that trouble would come if she opened up her shores. Japan, that long defended herself against global trade, its excesses and successes, its bounties, and its taxes. Hokusai uses a European hue, Prussian blue, and modern western perspectives to depict three fishing boats engulfed by a terrifying wave, with a Mount Fiji, dwarfed yonder, for scale. Japan's Edo period was one of isolationism and deep concern and cynicism towards external influence. Who knows what the waves off Hiroshima and Nagasaki resembled just over a century later when Japan's integration into worldly affairs reached its apocalyptic climax?

When we met, in the early part of this century, I was almost a womanizer as my primary occupation. Certainly, I spent more time fornicating than doing anything else. Except maybe sleeping. I f*cked myself to sleep and slept myself to f*ck. When we met in Edinburgh outside a comedy venue where I was pursuing my secondary function, stand-up comedy, itself a means to an end, she was radiantly nineteen. She was, in fact, a ridiculous beauty. She was all blondeness and bosom. Her hair looked like you could bite it. Like a horse's tail. She was like a delicious dessert in a camo jacket. What a wayward young fool I was, that could not see beyond pleasure and want, even when in front of me stood my future wife and the mother of my children. How blind and dumb I must've been, how wounded to not be able to see that far from being an object for me to distract myself with, to unthinkingly consume, here was the person from whom I would learn to be a man. And to learn steadfastness from, to learn loyalty, duty, kindness and fortitude. Selfishness has always come easily to me, that's what made me such a good priest for our fallen culture's warped creed. My wife is a native to heaven. Organically kind, decent, moral, good. Were I prone to regret I would smart at the decade lost in foolish self that, were I less of a fool, I could have spent at this magnificent woman's side. The Edinburgh Festival is to comedians whatever that place Coolio was describing is to gangstas. Insomuch as if you scrutinize it, you may emerge with questions but if you don't its brilliant. I could never tell if Coolio liked it there or not, to be honest. But paradise is paradise and what are you gonna do but chat to snakes and eat apples? Then my beloved wife, she would've, and there's no nice way of saying this, entered into rotation. That means that in the mix, on the unofficial roster, of the dozens of women I was hooking up with at any one time. It seems pretty revolting to admit, especially as I can hear my kids, her kids, our kids, on a trampoline as I type. But at the time, I thought it was great. As a salve on the wound of who I had been up until then it worked, with some obvious irony, like penicillin. Ironic because that behavior meant I sometimes had to take it. The tributaries and springs that contribute to vast oceans must share essential qualities with those awesome depths and in hindsight I can see that I loved her then. But I had mastered a kind of casual love, cheap love, cheap, fast love, a cheap, fast, well-packaged Mc-Love, that tastes great when it's in your mouth but may not provide the nutrition that you truly crave.

Laura had been long sought and courted by the great womanizers of our age, and she'd been rebuffing pop stars and national television sensations since she was about fourteen. There's a weird thing in English culture where barely pubescent girls go to nightclubs disguised as adults and get with footballers or whoever. It used to be, alarmingly, celebrated.

As I believe is usually the case, she knew before I did, she chose me early on, and thankfully, was willing to wait while I went round the world with my pants down and my mouth open like Ozzy Osbourne snorting ants. Fortunately, there were no negative side effects. Well, that's if you discount the provision of thousands upon thousands of opportunities for a highly motivated and biased media to later reframe these encounters as crimes.

In the UK, when newspapers publish what are known as "hit pieces" against you they give you a seven-day warning they're obligated to give. One came to me from the *Sunday Times* and Hard Cash, a Channel-4-funded production company, working together in an unprecedented collaboration, if not conspiracy. It fizzed with grandiosity and pomp, likely to mask that, in essence, was a series of attacks—including somewhat legitimately, a critique of my antics at the aforementioned Community festival, where I must be honest, I did march about like a bit of a goon. This was made much of. The most incendiary allegations in the hefty document, though, were eventually performed by actresses shot in silhouette in the Hard Cash show in the way that you see witnesses that testify against the mob filmed.

The week between being informed that these hit pieces were coming out and the actual simultaneous broadcast and publication was a stretched and thick time. Consultations with charge-what-they-want-by-the-hour lawyers, horrifying prognoses, difficult conversations with friends and family, emergency in-house 12-step meetings, phone calls from people who'd been through similar. It amounted to a kind of uninvited and unwanted death of self.

Most of my life, I'd never had to confront that I worshipped a constructed self. A set of beliefs and relationships that I lived within. A kind of internal program that is regularly affirmed externally. If you're famous, you acclimate to having a second self, a version of you that people know and respond to either negatively or positively (indifference can be in either of those categories depending on the context and how you feel that day, and sometimes you don't want to be recognized). I suppose that the womanizing became so prolific because if you're not excessively sybaritic there's not a lot else you can do with fame. Go out? Sit behind velvet ropes? Get free stuff? Who cares? Sex is at very least a lower chakra defibrillation and at best a voyage into a parallel reality where intimacy with a stranger serves as a fleeting facsimile for a brief and shared transfiguration. Once you're married and have kids it's best and frankly necessary to let go of that aspect of your identity and, for a little while, it seemed like I might be able to be satisfied with some Isis version of extreme domesticity: dog, cats, chickens, kids, thatched roof, row boat, a kind of grafted-on attempt to bleach out through twee pleasures and pastoral comfort. But without Christ, nothing makes sense and before long I was agitating online for revolution and once more in the company of names you'll now all be familiar with: Candace Owens, Ben Shapiro, Robert Kennedy, Charlie Kirk. In short, the new class that emerged from the explosive power of independent media. My inclinations are generally counterculture and trend towards truth, as best as I can determine and, inevitably, I found myself at odds with existing media and governmental power. I'm not suggesting any of this is connected to my forthcoming trial and it seems grand to make the claim that these coordinated, government-endorsed and exploited attacks were the result of my influence or power and there are times when even I doubt it. Then I look at the preceding months of media hit pieces, the attacks on other prominent independent media agitators, and it gives me pause. I'm sure Hard Cash (I mean, just look at the name) have no motive beyond helping people see the truth. So soon we'll see a a spate of documentaries about the people who actually did commit sex crimes: the visitors to Epstein Island—not all of them, as I'm sure some went for the coconut juice and to meet real life Mossad agents, but surely there's a documentary in it. Mainstream media cannot make objective documentaries about their hated rivals in independent media any more than Pfizer can conduct objective studies about ivermectin or vitamin D, or links between autism and childhood vaccines. They have a vested interest in the outcome. Thankfully, in the interceding years there has been abundant evidence of mainstream media companies meddling with content, from the BBC through to MSNBC, and no one in their right mind trusts them. This is what it's like when you're the middle of a media storm. As with meteorological storms, there's an eerie quiet at the center. Your home becomes a prison. Outside your house, paparazzi swarm. They smoke and click and coagulate, they shriek and spit. It is demonic. Of course, all the people that made money from you are spritzed into naught like oil in a hot pan. That's almost an instant benefit, as Julian Assange said, "We have superpower, we know who really loves us, most people never know that." If you have young kids, you have to make a game of getting them out of the house. Ours went to their grandparents. You have to have difficult conversations with them.

You have to employ security; whether it's to protect you physically or not, you certainly feel assailed. I had a show booked at Wembley arena and was counselled to go ahead and do it. It was like walking into the thick and scented air of a dream, nothing seemed real that night, or perhaps so real as to rinse away the suddenly less vivid reality that I'd occupied until then. The audience gave me an ovation as I walked onto the stage and I tried to work my way through my set but there must surely be a measurable component to attention, some kind of charge, and I could feel it bearing down. When the papers were printed and the show was aired I noticed how quickly the UK government jumped on it and said that I should be demonetized online. I observed how many actually pretty powerful people noticed that something odd was happening. Elon Musk, Joe Rogan, and Charlie Kirk thought plainly that the story was political, both in its intention, effect, and in the way that different people responded to it. One heartening aspect was to note how even people who claimed to be indifferent to me as a public figure, or sometimes even to dislike me, pointed out that in "our justice system" a person is innocent until "proven guilty." That the assumption is that a person who is accused of, or even charged with a crime, has the right to be assumed innocent until such a time as evidence can be presented that puts the matter beyond all reasonable doubt. I am not here proposing a connection between these events and my trial later this year. The BBC, Channel 4, the Murdoch press, and all UK media campaigned collectively and extensively for weeks to generate the collective impression of guilt. The staggering thing was: it didn't work. Of course, lots of people who don't like me enjoyed the upgrade in ammunition, and I was always a divisive figure, even when talking about pretty innocuous things. I got death threats way before I started saying we live in a one-party state controlled by corrupt oligarchs, manipulated by a lying media, exploited by global corporations likely governed by an evil cabal. Some people wanted to kill me when I did little but brag about threesomes and come up with cute euphemisms for my own genitals.

Ten years ago, anyone subject to a coordinated media attack would be dead in the bath. But now, because of changes that ultimately come from technology, it's not so straightforward. Whether it's Joe Rogan or Tucker Carlson or whoever the crosshairs settle on, there is now a significant demographic, probably over half of the media-engaged population, certainly over half of registered voters if the outcome of recent elections is anything to go by, that no longer trust the media establishment. There's an incorrect tendency to mis-categorize these findings along obsolete political lines. This is not about left or right. Early beneficiaries or at least expressions of this phenomena were not only left-wing movements like Podemos in Spain (left wing, YouTuber) or Syriza in Greece (basically communist) but also the Muslim Brotherhood in Egypt or more abstractly yet, Napster, the "free music" site. Andrew Breitbart famously said, "Politics is downstream from culture." But culture is downstream from technology. When Marshall McLuhan said, "The medium is the message," the media he was referring to was centrally owned and coordinated. The print and broadcast media have always been in synch with state objectives because, obviously, they are part of a cohesive system that requires (at minimum) that governments legislate in favor of elite interests and media mask that process. The flow of revenue between commercial groups and media companies, in addition to shared ownership, is but one facet of this. For the first time in history, we now have decentralized media, and it is extremely disruptive to a very effective and long-established model. Now you or I, if we have the skills, the balls, and the moxie, can challenge these interests just by telling the truth online, whether that's about something as innocuous as the behind-the-scenes shenanigans of our favorite sports teams or the galling, likely global, potentially murderous intentions behind the Covid-19 pandemic. Were it not for independent media, the intentions that brought about the pandemic would have been realized into law. Global bureaucratic bodies, like the World Health Organization, would have the ability to mandate vaccine-like injections, impose confiscatory tax, and censor national media, including broadcast, print, and online. That could still happen. This battle continues, will technology be used to create individual and community liberty—the message that this medium carry is, conversely—decentralization. Perversely, the economic potential that this tech brings with revolutionary and potentially decentralized apps like Uber or Airbnb is being brought into the old models of control. In just the field of communication—the creation of community—there is an arms race. Will the people use this tech to demand and impose control over their own lives and families, under God, or will a god-like government use it to ultimately control all trade, banking, communication, biometrics, attention, life itself? Satan's long-harbored goal to achieve god-like power, omniscience through surveillance, omnipresence through screens, and omnipotence through AI and social credit score systems is slouching towards Bethlehem to be born.

Day 5: *Willingness & Humility*

And God said, "Let the water teem with living creatures, and let birds fly above the earth across the vault of the sky." So God created the great creatures of the sea and every living thing with which the water teems and that moves about in it, according to their kinds, and every winged bird according to its kind. And God saw that it was good. God blessed them and said, "Be fruitful and increase in number and fill the water in the seas, and let the birds increase on the earth." And there was evening, and there was morning—the fifth day.

Genesis 1:20 NIV

We are now unlocking Real Life Force in Christ. Power is coming. He is real and he is here. The Lord is working and close to empowering us to be the people He always intended us to be. We must therefore be willing to let go of a lot of the deep habits of our former nature. Are you ready?

After that list and chat on day 4, you know a lot more about yourself and your limitations. The horizontal beam of the cross—human relationships—will help, we are made for them, but the vertical beam is where we access Jesus. We are broken, yet he loves us.

We can use the resources we have hitherto accrued to address what we now know of ourselves. We are idiots.

But so were the disciples.

Peter, lying, fuming, hubristic. John so needy and queenie. And Judas, well I'm not sure there's a way back for that guy.

We must apply the will thus far deployed in pointless sin in His service and it's impossible alone.

Alone, I think I could drift via chocolate and porn into sex and drugs in half an hour.

With Him, I can withstand being lied about, slandered, attacked, all in addition to my own inner brokenness and the failings I've confessed to throughout this book.

I feel his love and purpose and know that all else was always this.

That I was lost in the facsimiles of the counterfeit culture.

My biggest problem is pride (what's yours? You should know now). I care too much about what I think you think of me. This is because inside I feel "worthless." This is because of sin.

I have been worshipping a false god, me, and I know that I am weak.

Yet when I am in Him and he in me, I am, obviously, not separate from God.

Then paradoxically, all my mad little designs and weird despotism can be experienced as a connection to His Absolute Power.

It cannot be reasoned, it can only be felt.

I am selfish, He is selfless yet the ultimate Self.

You must, must read the Bible, it will teach you how to pray.

Identify the biggest obstacle you discovered in your list and chat. Was it Pride?

Was it self-esteem (thinking about yourself a lot, but not thinking a lot of yourself)?

Was it personal relationships? Wanting to write the script for other people?

Was it sexual relationships?

Was it money?

Was it security? What you need to be okay?

Was it ambition? Your own private plan for reality?

After your list and chat you have examples of all of them. Bring them before Jesus and Our Father now.

Almighty God,

Beloved King.

Dad.

Dad.

Alright Dad.

You are everything that is and could be and you love me.

Thank you.

Please Dad, God, Father, I pray that you make me willing.

Give me the fuel Lord, the energy.

Lord, I know I am not everything, yet you God gave everything for me.

My worth is yours and in you and my life is Yours and in You. Lord let me see life as it is. let me see You as You are.

Please let me be near You God, remove anything that is between us, dear Jesus.

The Sixth Day: Love & Justice

God created mankind in His own image, in the image of God he created them. Male and female he created them.

"You don't need to prove yourself to anyone, Russell."

Laura Brand

"See, I am doing a new thing! Now it springs up; do you not perceive it? I am making a way in the wilderness and streams in the wasteland."

Isiah 43:19

In the mad heights of the radical reevaluation of who I was, what fame and identity are, what my purpose is, what the past was, the Lord spoke loud. When Paul says in Ephesians 3:20 "Now unto him that is able to do exceedingly abundantly above all that we ask or think, according to the power that worketh in us," he refers perhaps to interventions of the nature that I am describing. I would not assume that the best way to reach a man who is in the middle of an international media-sex scandal would be via sudden heart surgery on his son but that is the method deployed, and it was pretty effective.

When you have a baby with a heart condition, you have to take them for regular checks. We were generally taking him to the famous and much beloved Great Ormond Street Hospital for Children, a kind of saintly and adored national institution. The cool kids call it GOSH. So that's what I'll be doing from here on in. When I was informed that our child had complications, my immediate response was, "I'm not going to Great Ormond Street. I'm not having a baby with tubes up its nose." By the time we first arrived at GOSH, I had already been changed by the strange, sad disappointments that accompany complications in utero. The moral challenges, the confrontation with unassessed prejudice and lazy presumption. Emmet Fox says that many of us have not reexamined our view of God since infancy and unconsciously are reliant on shallow and vague data, viewing God, understandably, when you consider the titles and pronouns, as well as the culture at the inception of the hermeneutics, a father, a patriarch, a kind of powerful human. As Fox observes, whatever God is, He is not human. He is not a "he." Plainly the creator of all reality, a tiny subset of which is observable reality, a yet smaller subset is, sensory reality accessible to humans, and smaller still yet within his creation is language. It's hardly surprising that language is an insufficient tool, but along with music, math, and art—and the best examples of any of those three include elements of the other two—it's the best we've got.

I didn't know the casual unthinking vehemence with which I rejected the idea of a child with an illness, deficiency, or disease until I pondered it and when I did, I felt like I could not accommodate it. I felt too weak and broken, too attached to shallow perfection—or at least normalness—to imagine myself as the parent of a child that wasn't normal, sufficiently superficially normal at least to grant me and my family inclusion into the vast, invisible clans of homogeneity. My wife steered me into a new perspective on these pervasive assumptions when she told me that seven months into her pregnancy with our son, she'd had a mundane exchange in a coffee shop line with which any woman who's had a baby will be familiar.

"Ah, are you expecting?'"

(This question is a gamble in quite another way, we all know that!)

"What are you having? Do you know?"

"No, we're gonna wait till it's born . . . "

"Yeah. Well, it doesn't matter does it. As long as it's healthy."

To which she wanted to reply, "Well what if it's not healthy?" which we already knew it wasn't. Now, because I know him, it feels rude to call him "it" and because I know what joy he has brought us it feels wrong to conjure up the complexity that existed until he collapsed it into the simplicity of love (which, by the way, is exactly what it's like to come to know Jesus) but Laura, who was always certain about him, said that hidden in that innocuous small talk is a set of happy assumptions about life that we can here unpack. That we are entitled to healthy lives and healthy children—certainly I felt that way, that unhealthy children are inferior, and I suppose by extrapolation that unhealthy children are expendable. Perhaps even unhealthy people are expendable, maybe even everyone is expendable if they are not useful. This is where rationalism can lead. It's very easy to reason towards optimization when you assume that you or your host culture know everything. When I arrived at Great Ormond Street, I realized how little I knew about anything. What teachers I have been granted in this time of apparent crisis, what kindness, what grace. In the mad, hot heights, assailed by fake claims where, if it were up to me, I wouldn't have left my house at all, our son had a checkup at a local hospital, Wexham, a place of deep suffering. These appointments had become somewhat routine to us already. They check the baby's blood and oxygen saturation levels (sats), which in the case of a child with heart complications will usually be low. The local hospital though didn't accept Laura's protest that for her this was "normal" and kept her and our son in for further tests. They kept them for four days in the end. During these four days, the attacks were at their height. The lane was filled with paparazzi. The papers were full of stories. Questions were asked in parliament. Television companies did self-serving internal enquiries. The police advertized for complainants. It was recently revealed, through a leaked memo, that the BBC, the state-funded media company, did four times as many posts about stories connected to me than on war or immigration. It was not easy to leave the house. I felt a dark serendipity in my solitude. God wants me alone, I thought. Here I am alone, under assault, my daughters are with their grandparents and my wife is in hospital with my son. My assumed method of suicide would be dog leash over a beam in the garage. The lead has a choke collar and a loop handle that you could thread the noose through as you lash it over the beam. Then you have a short tight noose that tightens when bearing weight and a good brace. If this seems dark to you then let me temper it with two, off-the-head reactions from my mates that I told at the time. My mate Mark said, "The beam is too low, your feet would reach the floor, you'd just be tip-toeing and coughing." Another mate, who had played a hangman in a movie, said that death by hanging, when done correctly (he said this like a connoisseur) breaks the neck and spinal-cord and that's what kills you, not asphyxiation. Though that will kill you eventually. Not long before this, a friend of mine who was a British TV presenter had hung herself after being hounded and vilified by the media. So, it was in the air.

I listened to the story of Joseph. His time in the pit, a type of death. I understood the necessity for deep surrender. Laura asked me to come to the hospital. I was driven by four security men, a boy band's worth. They could've been a boy band too; they were gorgeous, one of every color. We arrived in a car park at the back of the hospital. They've got my wife and son in a single room in pediatrics. I was wearing a hoodie and a mask. We have to walk through children's oncology. Past the six-year-olds twisted with cancer, the bald children, the kids in tented beds. The gray pinched parents in the gray grim light. The drawings by siblings on the wall. The crying. The Lord, He is calling us home, He is speaking to us, through our despair, He is calling us home.

Me and Laura had a laugh in there. Eating chicken my mate had made us. Not me, I was vegetarian then. I watched her walk in the car park while I held my son. I knew that something powerful and profound was taking place. We laughed about our security and the strained, ghoulish, and frankly cancerous sounding voice of the ward manager who spluttered, "Your son is very sick . . ." in such a gasping, cockney hack that it seemed like she might croak before her next breath. In the bleakness and anguish of this place and my self-centered suicidalism, the Lord showed me parents and children in the midst of real pain, which meant I could not take what was happening publicly seriously. Not that rape isn't serious, even being falsely accused of rape is serious, just that when you know that you are innocent but accused, it can be terrifying. Why is this happening? What will happen to me? All these pretty selfish questions are put into stark perspective when you have to look straight ahead and not let your gaze drift to the right to avoid prying on the private grief of a parent watching a six-year-old die.

Great Ormond Street wrought its holy havoc upon my un-rung heart. You cannot be in a place of such evident faith and devotion and not be changed. The nurses are devoted, the doctors, the parents, the orderlies, the kids, you yourself are now devoted to a higher thing. You, like everyone there, have realized there is nothing more important than the health of these children and together in wordless devotion you attend to the highest good. When you see the battle-scarred staff, the hopeful parents, the innocent and marked children a change comes over you. Who am I to say, "I'm not going to Great Ormond Street."?

Victor Tsang, who Dr. Oz helped us to locate, has the humble excellence of an exiled Tibetan lama. It's like meeting the Dalai Lama and then the Dalai Lama operating on your child's heart. There are plains of excellence unconsidered, unvisited until it is demanded.

After many preparatory visits and consultations, a day is set for heart surgery. In our case, this was accompanied by the avalanche of media attention on an ecstasy of horrors, affirmed stalkers having their grievances faithfully run as front-page news, friends of long standing swiftly departing, allies fleeing, county authorities claiming their mandatory right-to-privately interview our five- and seven-year-old daughters to see if they've been abused. The cargo of a lifetime's nightmares spilled across the gulf of my mind. All this actually quite reasonable in the instance I was a criminal of the variety concocted, but one example clearly displays the truth of our situation; a situation where, everyone, deep down, knows what's really happening. All but a few poor, recruited stooges. In the way when you hear of high-profile politicians, and I'm sure each nation has their version, I know the specific instances in the UK and US, attended parties and social gatherings at the height of lockdowns (house arrest) that they'd imposed. The question that arises is, "If you are imposing this lockdown and not observing it, you must know that the virus is not deadly or even dangerous, otherwise you wouldn't be having parties." Their actions revealed the truth.

When the folky, feminist, "let's support women" publishing company that had been publishing Laura's books dropped her on day one, much was revealed. Of course, it demonstrates cowardice and a lack of backbone but, as with the above pandemic example, the lack of character is no surprise. The revelation, as Laura explained it, is this: "They're dropping me because of these allegations. Firstly, if they believe that's true—it's not me that's been accused, it's my husband. And secondly, if they believe it's true, why are they not checking if I'm okay? Why are they not asking if I'm safe?" She continued: "They know it's not true."

All these messy revelations melt away when you see the parking space for hearses outside Great Ormond Street. God is so vastly articulate that he showed me in one giant real-time myth that fame is diabolical, sex is sacred, love and family are everything and in spite of a news cycle that statistically suggests you're the most important thing in the country, you and your feelings and your life are no more important than anyone else's. You're just another Dad praying in the chapel at Great Ormond Street.

The morning we took him in for surgery was pre-dawn dark and it rained gently—spitting, we say in the UK. He looked up from his pram in wonder at the rain as it landed on his face. We prayed before we left in the kitchen of the beautiful flat we rented a short walk from GOSH. Our daughters were elsewhere, with grandparents, I suppose. Like the Holy family, my wife and son and I made the short pilgrimage and moved between chambers at the hospital, various stations of prep, like a video game or any bureaucracy that you've ever been ensnared in. Like gas chamber guards or Group 4 security workers that now monitor the British judicial system, the people you encounter in children's hospitals have high inoculation to pain. In the best cases this makes them saintly, in the worst it makes them blank. I must confess to being in a state of such deep biliousness and unbelief that it may amount to a kind of disembodiment. Strip-lit room to strip-lit room, forms are exchanged assigning consent, statistics are cited: 5 percent chance of death, 10 percent chance of permanent damage, the heart may not close, "we may leave his chest open." Laura handled all that. We ascended in a service elevator large enough to carry a car from the room where forms were signed to a bewildering studio where the anesthesiologists waited. I am quite tall: six feet two, yet these men loom in blue scrubs like Mayan priests over the central slab. Peculiar forms, molds, and gels are strewn, to hold his body in place, I presume. Laura cradles her twelve-week-old son as the kind and avuncular head anesthesiologist holds a mask over his face; he squirms and resists before he goes limp, still. The tempo changes in the room. I suppose a clock has started. My wife and I turn and leave arm in arm in solemn and yoked cortège. We walk through the stark and bleaching light back to the vast aluminum lift and descend to the first room. We are alone now, and I sink to my knees as she folds into a plastic seat. As I see her breast milk bloom, as if from a wound through her pale top, the pain bleeds through. Even infants can't eat prior to surgery. Half numb, we wander back to the house, and she sleeps.

Laura must then have access to a deep maternal power. She sleeps and eats in this twelve-hour window provided by Victor Tsang's holy hands and when he calls to tell me, "It is done," I make the short trip back alone. When you've been publicly accused of rape and you're famous, you have to dig deep. You have to dig deep into the past and into the truth. You must find the rock, otherwise ordering a coffee could push you over the edge. In Great Ormond Street you must navigate the colorful wards; they are named after animals and adorned with the mandatory logos of donating corporations. You must climb stairs; you must absorb stares. You must know that you are already dead and that now Christ lives in you. My son is in intensive care; his chest carved asunder, tiny, like a loaf of bread or baby in a manger, wires spill from his torso in a mad spaghetti of preservation. His face masked. The room beeps and thrums. A tower of monitors stands at the side of his bed. A screen renders SATS and stats and scores and you learn the meaning of them all, I knew he would be okay because I knew God was talking to me through him. I knew his mother and I would be renewed. I knew we were being saved. Like anyone who knows our Lord, I have come to see His hand and His abiding love in all things. I begin to see how I was being shown that my life (my life!) was teaching me truth. No, Truth. That Christ is all and in all. That the world is not neutral, that sin is not individual acts of aberration, those acts are the observable expression of the state of sin which comes from being in "self." Twice in three months the Lord allowed me to return the Son to the Mother. "He's in intensive care and he's okay," I tell her.

Now is the time of vigil. Of sitting in the ever-beeping chapel of prayer. One by one wires and tubes are removed. New nurses come, each more beautiful than the last; they do care, intensely. They show you how to hold your son, as plaits of cable and tube hang from his heart and through his skin. You try not to think of those fraught few hours where his acorn heart beat outside his body as holes are closed and valves inserted.

Some days, pacing between the two places, I'd allow my shoulders to round and my head to drop. A couriers' office at the midway point usually had a fair amount of hustle and bustle. As I slouched by one heavy day a leonine courier with tumbling dreads glimpsed my disposition and hollered, "Chest out, Russell."

Oh, brothers and sisters, we are in a war.

A holy war and if you don't know you're in it, you're on the wrong side.

The world's institutions have been captured by evil, by the devil in fact, and without Christ he will capture you, too.

Not always through lurid sin like mine, not through Faust and power and glory and erections and red carpets and fast glory. No, the evil one would prefer you slump in inert despondency, sluicing your precious attention on one of his blue screens, bored. Oh

Lord, grant us clarity. See the plain insanity of porn, of foul food, of flesh for flesh's sake, see that abiding and abundant beauty is all around and that He would recruit us as His Saints and co-heirs. There is no neutrality, don't kid yourself of that. At Armageddon there will be no Switzerland. In fact, a quick glance at the Nazi gold and banking situation fast informs you that even in earthly affairs Switzerland ain't neutral.

In a way, knowing Christ is to know yourself as you are, not the iteration of yourself as patterned by this world. Poor, sweet thing I must've been, ol' Russ as a baby flung into this world, like you in innocence, like our Lord, His creative power suspended in an infant. The culture grasps and molds, directs and scolds. You may end up an accountant or jailed. You may end up a mother or a seamstress. You may chew your way through Hollywood (a psy-op, managed by deep state interests), a drug addict (a means of managing godlessness and your thwarted holy nature), a giddy lord of concupiscence (craving bodily intimacy due to lack of intimacy with Christ). All I have known I unknow now through Him, all I review through His abiding lens. I see how my whole life, your whole life, too, has been an instructional, that there is an unfolding.

When I read in Rick Warren's call to Christian life, *The Purpose Driven Life*—having never even heard his name prior to my suicide-adjacent encounter with his account of his own son's death—that I would have to get baptized, I was skeptical.

This, along with his other proposals such as read the Bible, join a church, seemed planes away from my intended trajectory. While my life was then, and in retrospect had always been, an unfulfilling slog, I was reluctant to consider that I might become a "run of the mill," "bog standard" Christian.

Baptism? Biblical scholarship? Join a church? There's something about these suggestions that sickened me in a way that "become famous," "do peyote," "meditate," and "screw around" never have. Why is that? What is so particularly appalling about Christ? Is it when the Mahatma said, "I like your Christ, but not your Christianity"? Was it my Nan, my least favorite Nan, my maternal grandmother who I felt compounded me in wounded grayness. Whose Christianity seemed to me at seven and eight and fourteen to be a chastening thing, the kind of Christ designed to irk John Lydon, a Christ that chides and creeps, not the perfect paradox, both punk and orthodox, that was revealed to me in pain and saved me.

I've never been comfortable here. I've cozied down in pink and brown and snacked myself nauseous on the forbidden. I've tried to build a life from the culture's blunt and filthy manual, as if it were an IKEA table; became a star and scrambled up the arid Olympus of Hollywood land. I've trekked round studio lots and rub 'n' tug joints and stared, unwell in stairwells. I've lived with chickens, dogs, and tots under a thatched roof and hugged my blonde and healing son to my chest. But it is not here that I, or you, will be absolved in this delicious and dementing exile.

Bear Grylls, a man so madly outside of this shallow, sinful time, it's insane we share a language, texts to say: "Let's get baptized."

Yeah, right! I thought. "Alright," I replied.

April 28 was still months away and I thought, and I always think this about the future: "It'll probably never happen." Like when we arrive at this future month or hour it will diminish and disperse like a neat and fallen tubular fuselage of cigarette ash. But no, sure enough April 28 came, and there it was: baptism day.

I've taken every drug that I've ever been offered. I never had a reason to say no. And none of them delivered what I ordered. Weed is too weak, booze is too gloomy-in-the-swill-guts, cocaine is jagged-shark-sharp and sinus-sluicing, crack is so fast in and out like a mouse trap, or doctor's prostate finger, that you barely have time to enjoy it. Heroin at least warms you through, like day-old lasagna, especially the first few times and at least grants oblivion, but LSD isn't LSD enough, ecstasy has got some nerve using that name, and all the good ones that have lately been invented came after the watershed of my abstention. Fentanyl, meth, and synthesized opioids and zombifying cannabinoids—that stupor precinct preteens—are all after my time. And as for this galling, jaw-dropping, ball-tightening new phenomenon of marketing drugs as "wellness" well, the mind boggles. MDMA therapy, weed dispensaries, and even ketamine, that shrill sound tunnel of a drug parceled up as wellness; it's as if the world waited for my abstinence before making drug use socially acceptable. Ayahuasca retreats, psilocybin workshops, crack city-breaks; in my day this was all considered a problem. I've not been so incensed since I learned that Tibetan monks were spending all their time watching porn and tossing off.

The truth is, no solution built on self or oriented towards it can prosper. So, would baptism be any different?

Bear Grylls came as Bear Grylls is, ready for action. He has no off switch and continues to "special-ops survive," SAS style, even in the home environment. He treated our cottage no differently than an Everest Base Camp or a cruel Arctic tundra. As soon as he arrived, he noted the fence wasn't high enough and that you could access the switch that activates the electronic gate by reaching over from without; "That's not effective," he dryly noted. Into the house he strode with copies of "Amazing Grace" printed out and slashed into impromptu hymn sheets, folded under his arm. "Those candles are too close together," he remarked as he shot through the lobby. "We'll do it in the river at sixteen hundred hours," he announced, glancing through the kitchen window, as if scanning for Al Qaeda. "Have you heard from the vicar?" I shook my head. "That milk is out of date," he intoned grimly and punched it into the bin.

The vicar had somehow disobeyed sat nav and was on the other side of the Thames at a pub's jetty. "It's only two clicks upstream," said Bear, "we'll take your rowboat." There was no question as to who was skipper, even though it's my rowboat. Bear was undoing knots and grabbing the tiller as I perched, bewildered, a hapless stowaway on me own vessel. Soon Captain Bear had *Daisy Poppets* (that's the boats name, which, I'll admit, it killed me to tell him) cutting through the river and arcing towards the pier and the waiting vicar like it was the opening titles of *Miami Vice*. The steep, triangular vicar and his beaming wife were folded in by Bear in a swift instant as if being snatched up from Dunkirk and we were back at mine and gathered round a piano as efficiently as if thwarting an embassy siege.

The vicar read, Bear played the heck out of the piano, of course, at one point pronouncing it "dangerously out of tune," looming into its guts like a field-surgeon and tightening a "capstan screw" with his teeth and inserting a "makeshift hammer-shank" made from an acorn.

My wife and daughters sang alongside my beloved brother Joe, for whom the Pope himself is literally not Catholic enough, while Bear plonked the keys into submission and sang the hymn in earnest. I began to get that kind of tickly throat sensation that you only get in important work meetings or church, where you first try to suppress a cough only for it to become an out-of-body experience, a cough so all-consuming your life beyond it cedes into irrelevance on the other side of the cacophonous hack. No one said anything as I continued to cough as the vicar put on, honestly, a full wet suit, including those little rubber plimsolls deep sea divers are obliged to wear, before donning the white dog collar at the neck. I recall April showers but that could've just been stuff I was coughing up and Bear—my dog, believe me, that got confusing; you don't need Bear Grylls and an obstinate Alsatian with the same name at the same christening, something is bound to go awry. "Down boy" and "in your basket" are not commands the head of the Great British Boy Scout movement can be expected to tolerate lying down. A makeshift pulpit, as portentous as any in Nineveh, was formed as the vicar wielded his Bible and Joe and Bear flanked me to the bridling lip of Old Father Thames. Coughing still, in we went, me and these two substantial, transubstantial men, into the oozing roll. The padre now has eyes and holy book aloft, as our feet sunk in the sludge. "Do you renounce Satan?"

"I do renounce him."

"All the empty promises of this world?"

"I do renounce them."

"All sinful desires?"

"I do renounce them."

"Then Russell, I baptize you in the name of the Father, the Son and the Holy Ghost."

Back and down I go into the old river that knifes through England's broad belly, the river that Londons and rolls, the river that Elizabeths and Oxfords its wild way back to the source, the river that Tilburys and holds old corpses and new treasure. Something, somehow, happened down there, down in the dirge of the Old Father. No man ever steps in the same river twice because both the river and the man are flowing and up I come, newly beloved.

Christ is the only mind-altering substance you can rely on.

Ol' Joe, though, took a hit down there—a chunk of old Hogarth's glass near sliced the little-piggy-that-stayed-home right off his tootsie. Bear did triage in a riverside instant. "That will require immediate attention." Later someone called it a "demonic attack." From nowhere I could identify, Bear produced a bottle of medical alcohol and removed and spat the cap. "Joe, the next ten seconds will require you to be a man," he said with brow furrowed, and poured the contents onto barely wincing Joe's muddy, bloody toe.

I'd been Christian for less than five minutes and already I was driving a wounded man to hospital with a vicar. Bear stayed back to cook steaks and inexplicably remove his wet clothes till fully nude in the kitchen, bearing all, including his "registered-as-a-deadly-weapon" genitalia, by which time, having previously ascended a small Hebridean cliff face, at his immediate rear, the both of us in kilts, I had already significantly encountered. I'll admit it was a troubling sight to behold as I dangled and fumbled with clips and ropes but, on the bright side, it did wonders for me vertigo.

"You were baptized by a man who survives in the wilderness eating only bugs," said my mate Roberto, intensely. But I have given up trying to be Jesus. I know now how obstructive my messiah complex was to my spiritual development. You can't get far if amidst all your high ideals and koans, all your reveries and hard-won wonders, you continue to harbor the one thing guaranteed to prevent salvation: an unconscious devotion to self.

In there, in that musty, guarded cleft, is where the devil owns you, is where the culture steers you. "If God is everything then god is anything," said Jordan Peterson. And that is what I felt at the flat, dead yoga festival I attended after being led to Christ. For all our straining dedication, if the central pole remains unbroken then redemption remains an unused token.

The signs were always there, Lord, I always knew that the problem was me and the solution was You. I always knew that you were beyond Elvis or Superman or Socrates or Alexander. That you were a man but also Son of Man. The world knows too, Lord, that you hold the sacred code, the golden key, the answer. Somehow even under all that is unholy, and there is so much that is unholy, You transfigure through the Golgotha dumpster and in holy, holy, holy pierced expiration hung, cleanse me and make me whole.

You made and saved the world and still found time to talk to me. When I was in that HBO show *Ballers* starring The Rock, and I had been entirely rinsed of enthusiasm, the kindly stand-in that I'd chat to as they lit the scene, who looked like me to get his gig, went on to play, well, portray You in *The Chosen*—allowing me, me of all people, the pleasure to say, "Jesus is my body double."

God, you have a sense of humor, and thanks to You, I have one too. Holy, holy, holy. It took the death of fame and the transformation of shame, the end of sex and suicide, the dissecting of my son for me to see Your face and now my beloved shadow self, spirit animal, beloved friend is deep in the fecund soil. I hear Your voice. Bear was the thread I pulled that led me to you. His was the lead I held that I planned to use as Judas did to choke out all my pity.

In the movie *Man on a Wire* the Frenchman Philipe Petit, and boy is that a French name, walked an illegally rigged wire between the World Trade Center's North and South towers. Hardly the greatest transgression practiced against those buildings and it says something of my Englishness that I, in spite of what has transpired, prefer the Saudis to the French. The film explains how a thick cable required for the stunt is affixed when you don't have the cooperation of the building management. Though they seem to have been most accommodating when it came to acquiring last-minute "planes hitting (and collapsing) a girder supported structure" insurance policy. But that's a story for another book. To get a connecting cable between the two distinct structures, to bridge the chasm, the disconnection that must be traversed by the heavy cable, an ingenious solution was found. An arrow is shot from the north tower to the south, with a reel of cotton attached and unspooling. As it flies, it trails, leaving a barely discernible thread connecting the two towers, to which coarser string is attached, then wire, then rope, then cable. Then the walker can traverse a path strong enough to carry his weight. The wordless German Shepherd is the arrow that bears the thread that leads all the way to a love sourced from God. How else could a dog transmit such love, such clarity, but mostly love? If it were connected only to itself, a self-contained system, a highly articulate explosion, 13.8 billion years ago, causeless and terminally unrelenting, where there would be no sense repenting, nothing to turn to or from. When you find yourself there, worshipping everything, or worshipping nothing, or yourself, who alone are worse than nothing, know that you are exactly where they want you. And where only He can save you. Let Him.

Day 6: *Love & Discipline*

And God said, "Let the land produce living creatures according to their kinds: the livestock, the creatures that move along the ground, and the wild animals, each according to its kind." And it was so. God made the wild animals according to their kinds, the livestock according to their kinds, and all the creatures that move along the ground according to their kinds. And God saw that it was good.

Then God said, "Let us make mankind in our image, in our likeness, so that they may rule over the fish in the sea and the birds in the sky, over the livestock and all the wild animals, and over all the creatures that move along the ground."

So God created mankind in his own image, in the image of God he created them; male and female he created them.

God blessed them and said to them, "Be fruitful and increase in number; fill the earth and subdue it. Rule over the fish in the sea and the birds in the sky and over every living creature that moves on the ground."

Then God said, "I give you every seed-bearing plant on the face of the whole earth and every tree that has fruit with seed in it. They will be yours for food. And to all the beasts of the earth and all the birds in the sky and all the creatures that move along the ground—everything that has the breath of life in it—I give every green plant for food." And it was so. God saw all that he had made, and it was very good. And there was evening, and there was morning—the sixth day.

Genesis 1:24 NIV

God, through Christ has given us everything we need. He has made us sovereign. We can through Him and with Him rule reality. If we are obedient to Him, faithful to Him. Are we willing to enter into the flow of His forgiveness and grace?

We are here to love one another and enjoy the forgiveness we receive by forgiving others. We can have no unforgiven people, places or concepts in our lives.

In our sin we have hurt people.

Our brothers and sisters in Him. We have separated ourselves from Him.

We cannot ever atone for what we have done.

He has by Grace, atoned for us. Accept His Grace.

To show we have believed and received we may become like Him, to receive Him, transmit Him, be with Him.

"The stoic's error is to assume he can do always what he can do sometimes."

Sometimes, by His Grace, I am pretty lovely, nice to people, fun, thoughtful, and kind.

Then, I dunno why or somehow even when, but I switch off and drift back into self, sin, in-Self.

We must make ourselves right with the world.

Use the inventory to identify anyone you have hurt, whether they have hurt you or not, and reconcile yourself to them in Truth and Golden Light.

This may require action and demonstration. Never undertake this without sanction from a believer to whom you have made yourself accountable in the preceding work. Maybe the person you shared your list with. Maybe someone from the church you by now attend.

Write here:

Who you hurt.

What you did.

What you should have done.

If it is possible to make in-person amends, do so. Always asking if you have missed something, or if they'd like to add anything. Remembering that of course, this is not you and them, this is you and God.

As Brother Lawrence said, "I live as though He and I are the only people in the world."

Which means to Brother Lawrence, all people and circumstances are God.

This is what we are granted through Love and Responsibility.

Be in His presence now.

The Seventh Day: Perserverance, Spirituality, & Service

God blessed the seventh day and made it Holy

"The privilege of a lifetime is to become who you truly are."

Carl Jung

"Be still, and know that I am God."

Psalm 46:10

> "God said to Moses, I AM WHO I AM. This is what you are to say to the Israelites: I AM has sent me to you." Exodus 3:14, NIV

And now Bear, the dog with whom I walk when thoughts of suicide come and go, has died. Yesterday we set the space for his departure. Spontaneity—which is evidence of God in the present—directed his funeral. At the front of our new home where we live, at first in exile but now anointed and ordained, there is a generous forecourt with encircling trees that invites a shrine. The unfolding of time reveals purpose like a life lived backwards. Deep in the soil he is buried now; the last time I typed he was at my feet. We don't wear masks with dogs, maybe with all pets. All pets are portals, nature's channel to nature's source. In the winding and paralyzed last days, as I sob on my knees, he on the bed, as if before me on the altar, I note the impulse to modulate even my cries; as yawning grief rears, a hundred infinitesimal tracheal checks might be instantaneously and unthinkingly imposed. If I cry in front of my wife, I may lean angrily in. My children I may assert restraint. A male; I may stifle or groan or otherwise embellish this most involuntary grief. And as I sense these long-encoded spasms inflect through peristalsis in the upward-rushing-mourn, some "inner witness me" advises, "What's the point? He's Bear, he's your dog, you can't through masks or manipulation affect him in anyway," He is who he is. "I am who I am." So, I just be who I am, and cry how I cry. He was on the walks in the dark darkness of the darkest days where I asked my god then, which perhaps like all pagans, was me, a nexus and web of impulses and projections and misinterpreted divine interventions. He was there when I asked the darkest of questions, "Lord, oh lord of self, oh, reified, ignoble yet dignified me, inverted I AM, 'you are' would I exchange my unborn son's life for my ongoing identity? Lord, would I? Would I prefer my son die than I endure these trials? And the One True God puncturing and un-lovely showed me, 'No, you don't want that. You don't love your cage of idols so richly that you would exchange it for your son.'"

In Seligman's famed experiment, caged dogs are exposed to

electric shocks. Group A has access to a lever that alleviates. Group B does not. Group A learns to use the lever, Group B learns to live with the discomfort of shock, lying down and taking it. Eventually both sets are put in a cage that emits a current but that can be easily escaped. Group A escapes, Group B just takes it.

All of us are in a cage of subtle shocks, all sensory information is transduced into neurological electricity before it is received by the brain. There are chemical hurdles that are overcome as synapses are crossed, mysteriously, like the Red Sea. All of us are, as Shakespeare said, subject to the "heartache and thousand natural shocks that flesh is heir to." All true geniuses are mystics, and the mystic is able to be ("or not to be") in the present. The present is where the living God is found. The dog invites you to be (or not to be) in the present, because your identity is a conglomerate derived from the past and all else is mad conjecture. Shakespeare knew like a dog knows that amidst all the difficult to detect, hard to explain neurological activity is a phantom deeper yet. The self. The self that Dawkins, and all the pious atheists believe is just a sum of the parts of a self-contained and highly articulate explosion, 13.8 billion years ago. But the dog knows. And in my dream of grief I know, too. I know that time is not real, and the persona are not real, and the lines upon which they shuttle and hurtle are not real. The temple, Solomon, the space cut off from time and stretched across it, is built at the site of your greatest wound, if you repent, David. You must sacrifice the most important thing to you, knowing it is God's anyway, and if you are willing, God will take care of you, Abraham. For the Christ will come and the man of living earth will live by spirit and breath and die on the cross to return you, you dear reader, to your original and intended state. Walking with him in Eden.

All these events occurred in the same place. This tells us something about time, about the temporal. And you may splutter your bitter brew and yell "of course they happen in the same place, this data is derived from documents compiled in one geographical region . . ." but surely, even as the bile still flies you'd be inclined not to deny that electrons separated by any distance laugh in the surly face of time, reversing their charges at times periphery, whistling gentle breezes up the petticoats of certain and metronomic atomic clocks. Surely as the foam coagulates and dries in the corners of your mouth—"How, God, how?"—you'd be inclined to wonder why the mind makes particles and the unmind makes waves. Why possibility exists until collapsed by certainty. Why the interruption pattern in the double slit suggests that, unobserved by man's collapsing mind, the particles pass through and around the slit, yes and no and both and neither, all at the same . . . time.

The same game of love and sacrifice plays out again and again, through and around apparent time. Could anything be more solid, fluid, blunt, and soft than, "I AM"? Unbounded yet signifiable.

God, the unmind, the all mind, the all possible, always, the I AM, put those events in that place to show us that time is not real to He that is outside of time.

"It is finished." John 19:30

When Christ expires, returns His spirit, his breath, the breath that Yahweh uniquely gives to Adam, the dirt man, then it is done. Time is velocity and entropy observed. The root, the source, the prima materia is spirit, not separate from its (His) Creator.

The wage of sin is death. We leave unity consciousness and its edgeless bliss when we yield to disobedience at the behest of the serpent. The serpent is sin. Sin is the frequency of separateness. It is dualistic, it is diabolical. The sibilant serpent *ssSSss*, the "s" sound, is voided of vocality and vitality and all of the "*vvvVvvv*" resonance, connectivity provided by the vocal cords, the inner instrument. The Virgin brings forth the reconciliation. The frequency of atonement at-one-ment is vibrated forth when the Holy Spirit, breath, incepts flesh. The serpent, the basal ganglia, invites you to separate, to disobey, to truncate faith and creating a temple to self, a time and space cut off, stepping out of truth. When the neuroscientific model that gave us terms like "lizard brain" was concocted they still ended up with a trinity, deliberately or not, the model was known as the triune model. God is real. Jesus came to atone for our sins; it is only knowable as a story in the mind of man because that's all the mind of man can handle.

No one will ever know how much I love Bear, you have to be me to know that.

No one will know how much God loves you, you have to be God to know that.

Even in these first hours of giddy-grief I felt the frosty and ridiculous prod that goes, "A dog? All this for a dog? That you can make your way to God, to Christ on the cross through a dog?" What is this book then? A long and profane palindrome? From dog to god? Is all we have to do reverse and capitalize?

Then my loving God bade me, "No."

"What type of dog was Bear, Russell?'

"A German Shepherd."

"A German?"

"Shepherd."

"Do you see it now, Russell?"

"The Lord is my Shepherd."

"The LORD is my shepherd; I shall not want. He maketh me to lie down in green pastures: he leadeth me beside the still waters."

"He restoreth my soul."

"He leadeth me in the paths of righteousness for his name's sake."

Psalm 23 selected pieces.

Only on the day he died, as I removed the hoodie adorned with this psalm that I'd unknowingly worn. Only as I thankfully watched unbidden friends and neighbors dig the five-foot pit, the teen daughter (I want to write virgin but is that too redeeming?) reading Matthew. Bear tries to drag through his paralysis, his last streak into his dug grave, burying it for a later he cannot know on this plane. The vet who is coming to administer the lethal injection is late and by then our playlist has lapsed, and our spontaneous guests have departed, and Prodigy plays and candles are lit, and the glorious and insane dog is lain by his own grave. The wild and broken dog. The dog that made the papers when he slayed sheep—"the worst celebrity dog in the world," but what do they know? He's not a dog and I'm not a celebrity—and Courtney Love's Pomeranian came in about third, the little bastard, I personally know two people bitten by that fiend, my own daughter among them.

I was surrounded by suicide back then, in my last pilgrimages, as a lapsing pagan. The man at Hambleden marina, Mark, unremarkable to me, unremarked himself to death on a steep tree in high Christmas a year earlier. He always seemed so nice. So stable, lacking even the glamor our filthy culture would attribute to self-slaughter. Like the dad at the school gates, nice bloke, got me a coffee when he saw, a few places behind in the line, that I'd reached the till without a card. He, too, hung in a lonely wood. It's all too much or not enough. And I was about to take the middle noose between the two, when you Lord, my Shepherd, on that walk, in that valley carved by time, on that pasture, by those still ancient waters, the Thames, sat down, folded really, and held Bear's leash and noted its easy geometry. When Ralph, Ralph from NA (?) Ralph, QPR Ralph, Ralph who had Gareth Southgate on a 12-step inventory for missing a penalty against Germany that led to him smashing up a pub, that lead to him getting banged up. Ralph sent Rick Warren on a Christian, yuck, TV show with them pair of televangelists all smiles and tax breaks. and Rick Warren told the story of his son's suicide in a way that I know now was Holy, set aside, set apart. Set apart from what? From porn cinemas and banks? No. Set apart from time. Before the fall there was no time. There was no decay. Decay is time. Molecules move apart, away from unity. The serpent has no vertical axis. He slithers, sibilant *s*, all separate breath in 2D. Satan, that ancient snake, wants a kingdom apart from you Lord.

> "Yea, though I walk through the valley of the shadow of death, I will fear no evil: for thou art with me; thy rod and thy staff they comfort me." Psalm 23: 4

A sage told me, "I'm not sure I'd stay in a country that was trying to kill me," so I left the UK with my family. We landed in Georgia, named for King George, the earthly king, in a hurricane. I went to D.C. to orate in the capital of your democratic republic. We found refuge in the panhandle, the trigger of the Florida gun, the state named by Ponce De Leon for the "flowery Easter feast" that heralded his arrival there. When we landed, we found along the Emerald Coast a community of God's people waiting for us and a land we could put our stake in.

The vet is late, and I consider again my gun. But she comes through the thin delirium of these last minutes. She issues the opioids as Buckley plays and I see his head get heavy. She doesn't tell us that she hasn't found a vein so the lethal injection is sluicing fruitlessly through his passive and respiring body as his tongue lolls in the dirt. Twice more she comes, he didn't want to leave us; he came to bring us here. He came to be buried in the soil to feed the magnolia tree, to give our home a center, to give our family a shape. To make sense of our name, Brand, the logo burned in by fire. We put our Shepherd, our stake, our sacrifice into the ground. And Bear, god love him, and surely God does love him, put his steak in the ground, too, one final heartbreaking, heartrending, life-affirming, after-life affirming act, the dog that shepherded me from selfish manhood into the arms of Christ, attempted to bury one last bone, his last grave-side meal, in a hole we'd dug for him, for a hereafter we may yet by faith alone, know.

> "Thou preparest a table before me in the presence of mine enemies: thou anointest my head with oil; my cup runneth over. Surely goodness and mercy shall follow me all the days of my life: and I will dwell in the house of the LORD for ever." Psalm 23: 5-6

Next time I go to the UK, that most disunited and fallen kingdom, it will be to clear my name. But it's not my name anymore.

I don't belong to me, I never did. And neither do you, you belong to Him. The word, the light, the truth and the way, the one that came and died to take on your sin, because He loves you so much, even though you are wild and broken. You can never conquer time and all that time has wrought; you can never conquer the world. But fear not, for in you is one who has conquered the world and He is more powerful than the dark forces that control this one.

Day 7: *Perseverance, Spirituality, & Service*

> Thus, the heavens and the earth were completed in all their vast array.
>
> By the seventh day God had finished the work he had been doing; so on the seventh day he rested from all his work. Then God blessed the seventh day and made it holy, because on it he rested from all the work of creating that he had done.
>
> Genesis 2:1 NIV

Can we be with God as He always intended? In spite of all you have been through and in spite of all your brokenness and sin, the answer is yes, through His Son Jesus. Rest in Him, abide in Him.

This is your life now. stay aware, surrendered, hopeful, loving, be of service and observe how "the evil one" guides you into sinful states. The state of separateness.

The only solution is salvation.

Now there is nothing else. "You are already dead. Now live properly." Marcus Aurelius.

"Don't pick up the corpse." Buddhist maxim.

"For I have died on the cross with Him, it is He that is reborn in me." Saint Paul.

There is nothing to get, yet everything to live for, you are His. You always were. It is there, in plain sight, the Christ. The God man, entering into time, like your spirit is in your flesh, the son of man entered time.

Live aware now, noting how the stimulants that charge your cage affect you and using all to move closer to Him.

The incredible and "oh, so simple" truth—that it makes a mockery of even writing a book—is, "Put other people ahead of yourself." That's it.

If you do that, when you are in God, He will enrich you, and when you are not, He will show you that you are not through your inability to do His will in the Grace He gave you. When I don't want to help people anymore I know I've let go of His hand.

Here is how you daily observe your state: Here is how you daily move closer to Him. Here are some people you can serve:

The world is in the thrall of the evil one. The point of the culture is to destroy you by stealing your soul. This, though, requires your participation, as does your salvation. The world, through your thoughts and flesh, has conquered you. But do not be afraid, for He who is in you is stronger than he who is in the world.

So:

Accept Christ as your savior.

Pray always.

Be in His church.

Get baptized.

Love His kids.

You are now a Christian, and so am I.

We will be together for eternity in paradise.

To better understand the work in this book and indeed to surpass it, please consider reading, in addition to the Bible, obviously: the *Big Book* of Alcoholics Anonymous, *Purpose Driven Life*, everything C. S. Lewis has ever written, Emmet Fox, first164blog, *Living Fearless* by Jamie Winship, Ruth Burrows, *Presence of The Living God*, *Course in Miracles*.

Acknowledgments

Bear Grylls for the baptism and for taking the heat. "Special forces" for the nation but mostly for our Lord. "You don't have to be SAS to baptize me, but it helps." Thank you.

David Bull for showing me the Message, telling me to read Acts, and revealing his vulnerability.

J John and Killy for their familial and dedicated instruction and nourishment. For their sincere prayer and mentorship.

Nicky and Pippa Gumbel for the bold instruction and clear, kind guidance. Especially for The Bible in One Year, which I lost on a plane after my second trip 'round and now know what it is to daily be in the Word without guard rails.

All Saints Church Marlow.

Tom, Miranda, and all who pray for me.

Debora and Clayton, prayer warriorship and stewardship.

My 12-step friends across the world.

Jimmy M, atheist cardinal.

Jeff, Jimmy, Perry, Rory.

James. Irons.

Gareth. Blimey.

Gee, forwards.

Mark W for the Wexham Park chicken.

Mick The Ferret.

Allscapes Mark. Thank you for your loyalty and instruction when it would be easier to walk away.

My parents, Babs and Ron.

My brave and astonishing in-laws. Thank you for your faith in me under extreme pressure.

Destiny Church. Good News Church.

Pastor David, Hayley, Bruce and Robbie, Phil, John, Mandy, Joseph, Rochelle, Phil, Richard, Larkin, Josh, and everyone at Christ the Redeemer.

Ajay Gupta, for your sound, kind, strong, and sensible advice.

Tony R, "hunter of human excellence."

Dr Oz and Lisa for shelter and protection and for mending broken hearts.

Secretary Kennedy for demonstrating character, strength, humor, and grace, and for showing us how to be victorious through righteousness.

Cheryl Hines for putting up with that crap.

Allie and the whole Smith clan. RIP Pops, Man of God.

Francesca Fields and her relentless brood.

Ken and Faye Stange for your gentle love and kindness.

Bobby J and Bev, surprise visits.

Kyle Via, priest, warrior aquatic hunter of depth.

Ang Heese. Earthed Christian.

Jonathan Roumie, Jesus is my body double.

Jeff Cavens, Catholic maker.

Claudio, Chris Pavloski, Jenna, Mike, everyone at Rumble. Thank you for streams in the desert.

Masseeh for making me look good.

Liam Sullivan, headhunter.

Charlie Kirk, RIP, "Romans is the Christian Constitution."

Hoberto F, Kibby, Mirabelle, and the boys for protection and for dottie.

Gary Brecka for bringing the light to so many, including Bear.

Nick Ortner for tapping us back to sanity.

M and W for the ongoing sanctuary.

The Browns, Sam, Nicki. Thanks for the deliberate and earnest work on this book, the observations on David, and for my beloved Gabe, Coco, and the boys.

Rick Rubin, wisdom, strength.

Summer Brown for the loaves.

Micheal Emmett, way maker.

Carlos Diaz. Survive, escape, control, submit.

Gary Thompson for taking the hits to the balls.

Chris Cleere for keeping me in the fight.

Chance and Erika, thank God you're at the end of our street.

Lara and Skippy for making the beach our home.

Richard and Susan for the steaks, Beluga, and southern hospitality.

Miro Sclavi, your father would be so proud. I am so proud.

Evan Lowenstein for his extremely valuable guidance.

Noel Fitzpatrick for everything you did for Bear and do for animals, you broken Saint.

Lucy Connor, white feathers often found. An angel now.

Lexi Ciccone for fitting me in between world leaders and golf carts.

Tucker Carlson, crusader, slayer of nocturnal entities, friend.

Oli Shneider Sikorsky, evidently positive, thank you.

Ian Winter, excellent advocacy in absurd circumstances.

Stacy Creamer, thank you for your help, in the present tense.

Adam and Brian, thank you for the insights and a cover that I'm happy to be judged by.

Tony Lyons, you are an activist publisher, a terrorist working in ink. I look forward to writing a book about you one day, with a flexible deadline.

Jerome Poubelle and Suz, thank you for the healing.

Bruce Lloyd and Bobbie. Riding shotgun. 911. Suicide prevention.

Jake Smith, my brother on the path and partner in mission and ministry. "Spark, light, reignite."

Dave Fields for leadership and for demonstration of His power through kindness, win-win mindset, and for keeping the chips rotating.

My brother Joe McCann, thank you for making my addiction seem reasonable and my life seem liveable.

Gavin de Becker, an army of words, a Normandie of gratitude. A Hiroshima of thanks. Oh no, is that reference radioactive because Yukimi is Japanese? There is one word I can't send into battle because it's a wound too hard to show (true story).

Mabel Brand, you made me a father, how wonderful to be your dad.

Peggy Brand, you show me who I am, little teacher.

Herbie Brand, my son. My beautiful son.

Finally, most importantly, of course, Laura Brand, my wife, my faith, my life.

What a family. What a journey. And we are only just beginning.

Praise Jesus. Who I meet in the eyes of all these people.

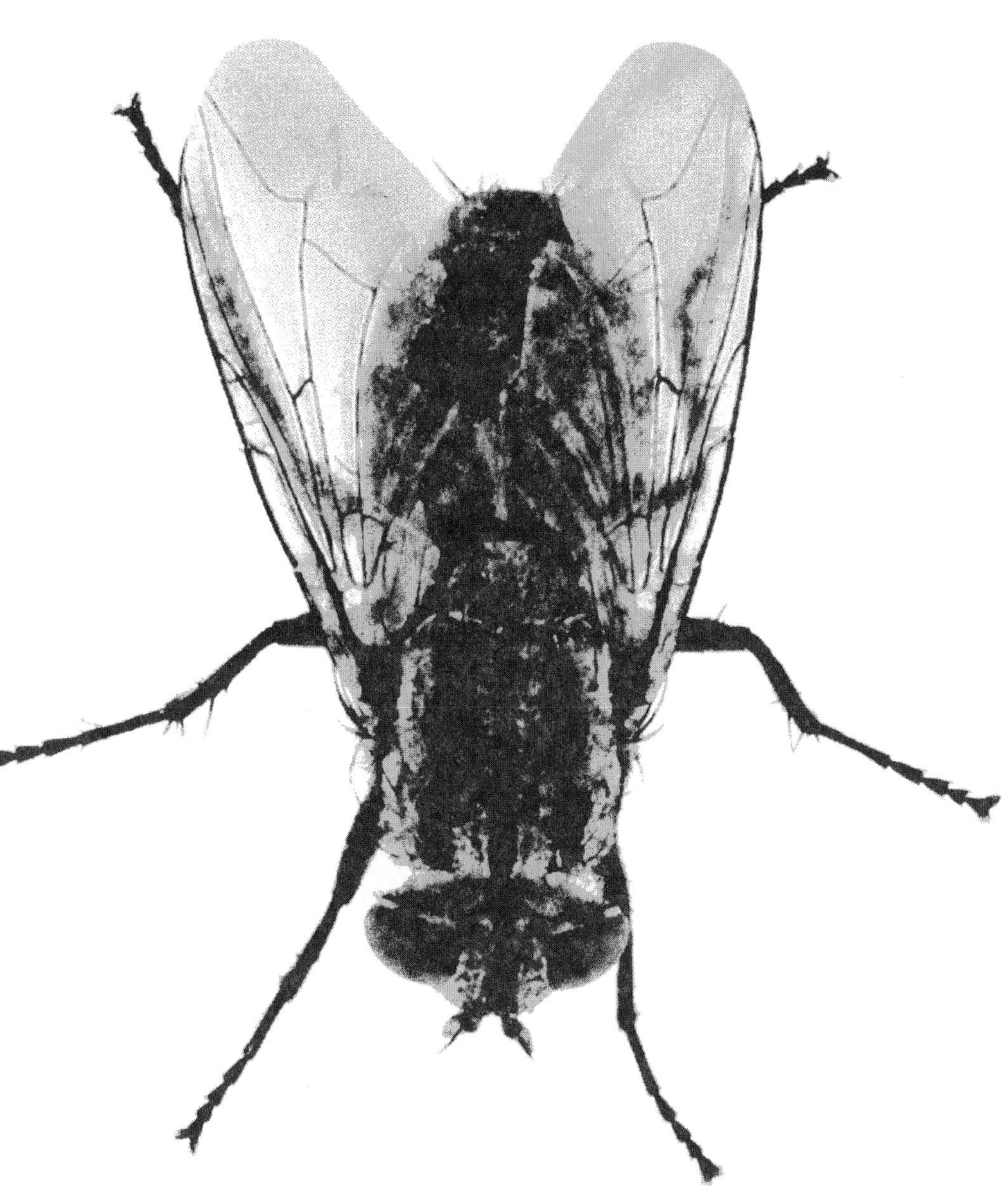

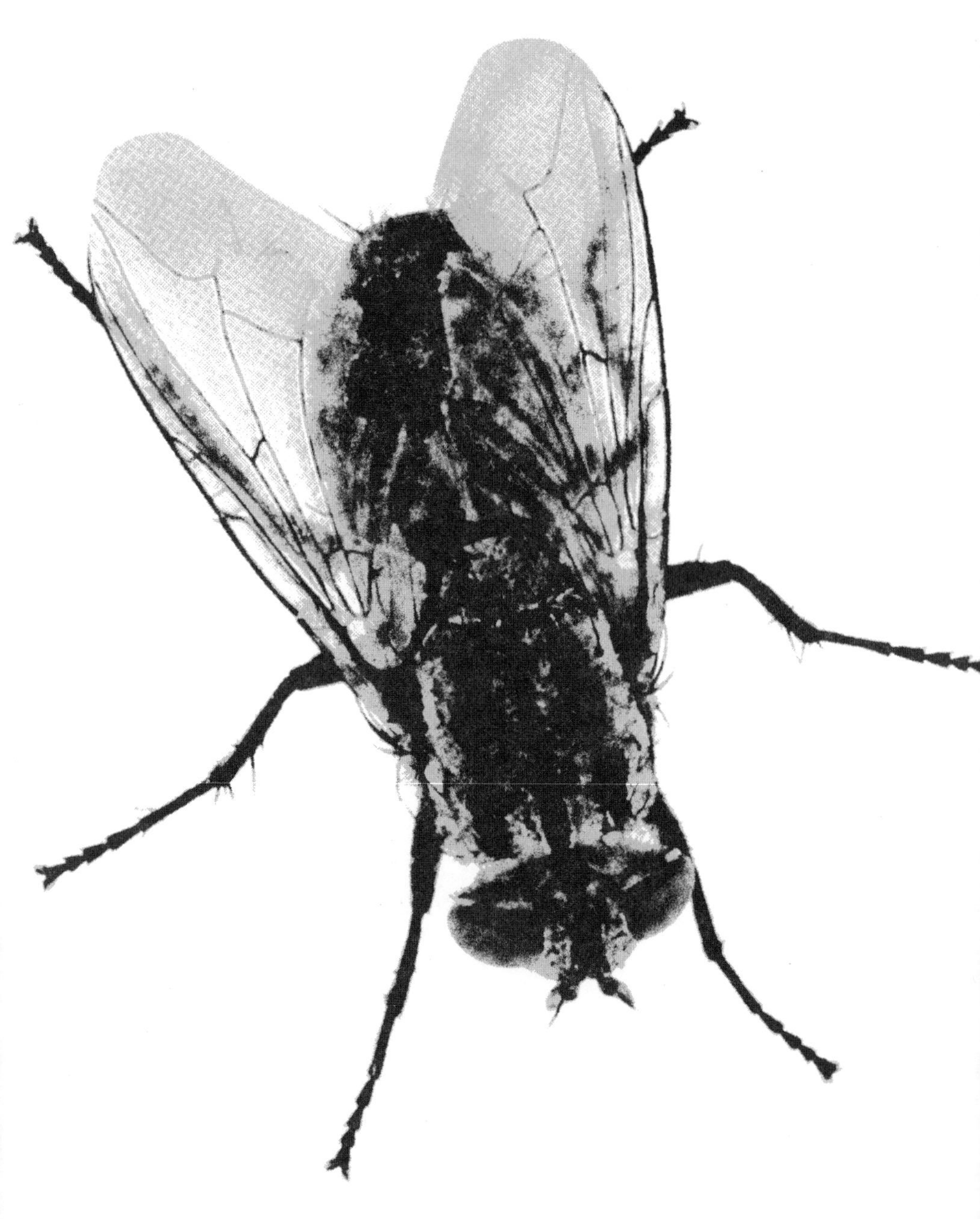